LIGHTFOOT OF
DURHAM

BISHOP LIGHTFOOT IN 1879

LIGHTFOOT OF DURHAM

Memories and Appreciations

Collected and Edited

by

GEORGE R. EDEN, D.D.

*Honorary Fellow of Pembroke College, Cambridge
formerly Bishop of Wakefield*

and

F. C. MACDONALD, M.A., O.B.E.

*Honorary Canon of Durham Cathedral
Rector of Purleigh*

CAMBRIDGE
AT THE UNIVERSITY PRESS
1932

CAMBRIDGE
UNIVERSITY PRESS

University Printing House, Cambridge CB2 8BS, United Kingdom

Cambridge University Press is part of the University of Cambridge.

It furthers the University's mission by disseminating knowledge in the pursuit of education, learning and research at the highest international levels of excellence.

www.cambridge.org
Information on this title: www.cambridge.org/9781107437838

First published 1932
First paperback edition 2014

A catalogue record for this publication is available from the British Library

ISBN 978-1-107-43783-8 Paperback

IN PIAM MEMORIAM
PATRIS IN DEO
HONORATISSIMI AMANTISSIMI DESIDERATISSIMI
SCHEDULAS HAS QUALESCUNQUE
ANNOS POST QUADRAGINTA
FILII QUOS VOCITABAT DOMUS SUAE
IMPAR TRIBUTUM
DD

BISHOP LIGHTFOOT'S BOOKPLATE

This shews the Bishop's own coat of arms quartered with those of the See, and the Mitre set in a Coronet, indicating the Palatinate dignity of Durham.

Though the Bookplate is not the Episcopal seal its shape recalls the following extract from Fuller's *Church History* (iv. 103):—'Dunelmia sola, judicat ense et stola.' "The Bishop whereof was a Palatine, or Secular Prince, and his seal in form resembleth Royalty in the roundness thereof and is not oval, the badge of plain Episcopacy."

CONTENTS

ILLUSTRATIONS

PREFACE

"THERE are many nineteenth century personali-
ties", wrote a recent reviewer, "whose lives and
characters are nowadays due for a revaluation."
There are few to whom this remark could be more fitly
applied than Bishop Lightfoot, of whom *The Times* wrote
on the morrow of his death: "The Church of England
has been too soon deprived of one of the greatest minds
by whom it has been served and adorned not only in this
generation but in its whole history....He was at once
one of the greatest Theological scholars and an eminent
Bishop. It is scarcely possible to estimate adequately as
yet the influence of his life and work".

It is the object of this book to preserve some knowledge
of the personality of Lightfoot while there yet survive some
of those who knew him intimately both at Durham and
elsewhere.[1]

There are happily several chance references to him
in the biographies of his lifelong friends, Archbishop
Benson, and Bishop Westcott his successor, and such

---

[1] Joseph Butler was one of Lightfoot's most illustrious predecessors, yet
only the most meagre traditions of his personal life remain. Bishop Phillpotts
of Exeter, who succeeded him as Rector of Stanhope, after eighty years' interval,
wrote to Archdeacon Goddard of Lincoln on Jan. 25th, 1835 "I earnestly
wish I could supply you with several anecdotes of Bishop Butler. The truth
however is that I have been mortified by almost entire failure. ("*Stanhope
Memorials of Bp. Butler.*" W. M. Egglestone.)

At Auckland Castle the searcher is little better off. There is a writing table
of cedar wood with "J.B." inlaid in brass given him by the merchants of
Bristol, and a silver coffee pot, and a defective Latin inscription, and a
tradition that he would stroll in "Butler's Walk" or sit in the Chapel to
listen to Father Smith's sweet-toned organ.

books as Bishop Forrest Browne's *Recollections of a Bishop*, and Mr A. C. Benson's *Leaves of the Tree*. There are some letters at Auckland Castle. And there is the most valuable article on Lightfoot in the *Dictionary of National Biography*—the last thing we have from Dr Hort's pen. And last but by no means least is the Article reprinted from the *Quarterly Review* of Jan. 1893. This is so masterly in its grasp and arranged so admirably under the heads of the Inscription[1] on the recumbent effigy in Durham Cathedral[2] that it must live as the best contemporary sketch of the great Bishop.

But something more is needed. He who did so much to direct men's attention to the Northern Saints should have men's eyes turned on him and his solid saintliness. His books reveal his learning and his extraordinary diligence: here, we may hope, stories of his daily life and intercourse may tell something of his character, albeit the beauty of inner life must remain unseen.

Bishop Westcott once expressed the wish that "there were some adequate record of his part in University affairs". This desire is met, at any rate in part, by Bishop Moule, his old pupil, who was afterwards to succeed him at Durham.

It is right too, that something should be told of the

[1] + In Memoriam Josephi Barber Lightfoot S.T.P. Episcopi Dunelmensis Natus A.D. MDCCCXXVIII, Obiit A.D. MDCCCLXXXIX. Qualis fuerit antiquitatis investigator evangelii interpres ecclesiae rector testantur opera ut aequalibus ita posteris profutura + Ad majorē Dei gloriā. Am. Pon. Cur. +"

[2] Bishop Westcott was once asked what he thought of this recumbent effigy as a likeness to his predecessor. He said "I have never seen it." "But, my Lord," he was answered, "you were there when it was dedicated, and you could not stand in your Throne without having it straight in front of you, just below." "*I have never allowed myself to look at it*" was his reply, revealing at once his extraordinary strength of will, and his ceaseless devotion to his friend.

origin and growth of the Auckland Brotherhood. Bishop
Westcott wrote:[1]

> If I may speak from my experience during the last three years, I
> believe that his greatest work was the Brotherhood of Clergy whom he
> called to labour with him in the Diocese, and bear his spirit to another
> generation, greater than his masterpieces of interpretation, greater than
> his masterpieces of masculine and passionate eloquence.

These words were written after three years of observation.
Those of us who have been members of the Brotherhood
for more than forty years could find no words to describe
better what our Father in God was, and still is to us.

As years have passed, our φιλαδελφία has expanded
into ἀγάπη, and we are glad to place on record our debt
to what so many have described as "far the greatest
influence in our lives".

The sermon which stands here as "The Epilogue" was
the foundation on which this book has been built. Archbishop Lord Davidson had expressed a wish that it
should be published, and it was considered by us all as so
valuable a review that we agreed that reminiscences
should be gathered to it, and put into book form.

We have thus a mosaic of memories the result of team
work of men bound together in love as Lightfoot's sons.

Among our contributors and helpers not mentioned in
the text, are Dr E. A. Welch, the Bishop of Durham,
the Bishop of Oxford, the Bishop of Southampton, the
Bishop in Argentina, Bishop G. L. King, the Dean of
Windsor, Canon D. S. Boutflower, Canon Alfred Boot,
Rev. H. H. Birley.

Some subjects which claimed his attention we have
deliberately omitted, for our aim is not to attempt a

[1] Prefatory Note, *Bishop Lightfoot*. Macmillan & Co. 1894, p. ix.

Biography, but rather to give word pictures from different points of view of the Bishop as we knew him.

Our pages will also endeavour to shew something of his mind as revealed in his writings, and the influence of his utterances on his contemporaries no less than his contribution to the Theology of his day, his place among Church leaders, and his lasting value as a Teacher.

We must also place on record our thanks for permission to quote from books published by Messrs Macmillan, Messrs Bowes and Bowes, Messrs Constable, Mr J. P. Jamieson, Mr W. M. Egglestone, *The Classical Review*.

G. R. E.
F. C. M.

1932

INTRODUCTION

WHEN Sir Walter Scott visited Auckland Castle in 1813, riding thither with his son and daughter, he made the acquaintance of Bishop Shute Barrington. They were so pleased with each other that the Bishop ordered his horse, to accompany them, and Scott observed with admiration its proud curvetting. "Why yes, Mr Scott", said the gentle and high-spirited old man, then in his seventh-ninth year, "I still like to feel my horse under me." They parted after a ride of ten miles with mutual regret.[1] The contrast between the leisured morning gallop of the venerable eighteenth-century Prince Bishop, and the ceaseless labours of his modern successor is no greater than the contrast between the days of Bishop Lightfoot and to-day. Though the difficulties he faced were quite as grave and pressing as the modern problems of unemployment and shortage of clergy, they were difficulties of a different order.

The grand Northern Palatinate with its leisured and dignified clergy had been invaded a generation before by the flood tide of industrial revolution. When the stage coach disappeared before the railway train, and peaceful farms had suddenly become pit villages, hardworking clergy and devoted laymen had alike been unable to adapt their ways to modern conditions. But an attempt had begun to be made, and when the new Bishop came he found the way opened for a great advance, and eager hearts waiting for a leader.

[1] Lockhart's *Life of Scott*, II, 231.

He thus describes the situation in his opening speech at his first Diocesan Conference:

The zeal, and devotion, and business capacities and the untiring energy of my predecessor were fitly expended on the internal work of the Diocese. In addition to the current duties of the episcopate—an ever-increasing burden in a large and growing Diocese like this—it was his special work to develope the parochial system by the formation of new districts, by the building of churches and parsonages and by the increase of the clerical staff....

In his last charge, delivered a few months before his resignation, Bishop Baring expressed his opinion that this particular work, the formation of new ecclesiastical districts, had almost reached its limits. This may be so, though as yet I see no signs of flagging....But a Church is something more than an aggregate of distinct parishes, or isolated congregations. The idea of a Church involves the conception of a corporate life. A Church is only a Church in so far as it realises this conception. To extend the sympathies and motives of common member-ship beyond the limits of the parish to the limits of the Diocese, is to make an important stride in the realisation of this idea.[1]

To make this important stride was Bishop Lightfoot's chief endeavour, with results that still bear witness to what God wrought by his servant.

His episcopate has often been called "The Golden Age" of Durham, and splendid it assuredly was. He was a great man, sent to meet a great opportunity.

But it is essential, in estimating his work, to bear in mind the extraordinary changes that have come over England since his day. One shrewd observer remarks that "the interval since Lightfoot has been perhaps the most revolutionary in our history, with the possible ex-ception of the Reformation". In every sphere, political, economic, academic, ecclesiastic, and local, there have been astonishing changes.

Three Franchise Bills have completely remodelled the electorate, and "Labour", now such a powerful force in

[1] *Durham Diocesan Calendar*, 1881.

England, and especially in Durham, was unheard-of in the eighties. Times of great depression they certainly had, coming at regular intervals, but nothing to compare with the stagnation and unemployment that paralyse industry to-day. Again, both in his charitable generosity and in the maintenance of his great position, Lightfoot, were he now living, would find himself handicapped by the altered value of money. Rates in his day were very low—Income Tax could be stated in pence; there was no Surtax, and no death duties. He would nowadays have to pay at least £1500 a year more in taxes. Wages were low and commodities such as coal cheap enough.

These and many other changes which have combined to make the work of the clergy of to-day more difficult even than it was forty years ago must be continually borne in mind in the reading of the following pages.

Preaching in Durham Cathedral on the Festival of Founders and Benefactors on January 28th, 1926, Bishop Eden of Wakefield took Bishop Lightfoot as his subject. In the course of his sermon he said:

Words are useless to convey any impression of the new life which sprang up in all directions under his inspiration and guidance. Vast schemes of Church extension seemed to grow up like magic; new Parishes, new Churches, Mission Districts all alike were the fruit of his unstinted generosity and of the willing support of Churchmen.

It is not too much to say, and as one who knew the Diocese before he came I dare to affirm it, that Bishop Lightfoot left a mark in the Diocese, such as few, if any, before him had done.

Thus we are able, by viewing the "Golden Age of Durham" from behind it, and from afar in front, to see its great Bishop in his true perspective. Times change and customs alter, but character remains; and the greatness and the humility of Bishop Lightfoot will be an abiding inspiration for generations to come.

Chapter I

EARLY DAYS, CAMBRIDGE & ST PAUL'S

JOSEPH BARBER LIGHTFOOT was the younger son of Mr John Jackson Lightfoot, a Liverpool accountant, and was born at his father's house, 84 Duke Street, Liverpool, on April 13th, 1828.

His mother was a sister of Mr Joseph Vincent Barber, a Birmingham artist of considerable repute. Of the three other children, an elder brother William Barber, six years older, took his degree at Trinity, Cambridge (Wrangler, and 2nd Class Classics), and was for many years Head Master of the Grammar School at Basingstoke, and later Vicar of Cartmel Priory in the Diocese of Carlisle.

One sister married the Rev. William Harrison of Pontesbury. The other, Miss Lightfoot, often visited the Bishop at Auckland Castle.

The future Bishop was a child of the North. His father was a Yorkshireman and his mother originally came from Newcastle, where his great grandfather had a notable bookseller's shop next St Nicholas' Church—the present Cathedral—in Mosley Street.

Speaking at the Guildhall, Newcastle, on July 2nd, 1881, Bishop Lightfoot said:

Whenever he came to Newcastle to preside at a meeting, it was always a satisfaction to him to recollect that the name by which he was known in Newcastle—Joseph Barber—was one he had inherited through four generations from a worthy citizen of Newcastle.

Shortly after this he restored the tomb of his ancestor in

the graveyard of the Cathedral. A new stone was made
with the old inscription:

Here lieth the body of

JOSEPH BARBER

late of Amen Corner Bookseller
who died July 4th 1781 aged 74 years
and of Eleanor his wife who died
December 25th 1784 aged 67 years.

The rest of the slab records the names of Mrs Humble
"daughter of the above" and her husband and children.
The discarded stone lay a yard or two away in the graveyard.[1]

As a child Lightfoot was delicate, and took little part
in games, though in later life he was fond of walking, and
was one of the first to ascend the Jungfrau in Switzerland
from Fiesch in the Rhone Valley, with only a local shoemaker as his guide.

His first public education was at the Liverpool Royal
Institution under Dr Iliff. After about two years here, he
lost his father and moved with his family to Birmingham
at the age of fifteen. Even then he was a good scholar—
equally proficient in classics and mathematics. He is
described as a boy of immense capacity for work, cheerful
temper, dry humour, and above all of reverent and disciplined piety. At King Edward's School, Birmingham,
he formed a lifelong friendship with Edward White
Benson, who was to become Archbishop of Canterbury,

[1] Mr R. Thompson, Senior Verger, Newcastle Cathedral, writes, Feb.
13th, 1931: "The Joseph Barber gravestone is to be found at the East end
of the new Library under the East window. The stone recut by the late
Bishop Lightfoot's instructions is in excellent preservation. The discarded
stone which had laid by the side of the grave has been used as a base for the
pillars of the newer stone, to prevent them sinking into the ground. This was
done in 1926 and will preserve them for many years".

and later at Cambridge with Brooke Foss Westcott, who was to succeed him in the See of Durham.

All three owed much to one of the greatest teachers of his day, James Prince Lee, afterwards first Bishop of Manchester, to whose lessons on the Greek Testament Lightfoot confessedly traced his enthusiasm for those studies in which he became pre-eminent.

The reminiscences in *Salpisei*[1] give vivid glimpses of the boy Lightfoot on the threshold of his vast treasure-house of learning. Later as a young Fellow of Trinity he writes:

I recollect when I was placed under his care, Prince Lee's advice to my friends was "Give him the run of the Town Library". We learnt by experience that any knowledge we might acquire would be brought out some time or other to illustrate our school work.

When I told him I would take Holy Orders he replied beseeching me to decide at once, and seek a curacy, or a mastership, or at once to begin to read and edit or write if I looked to Theology, for he added "Virtus in agendo constat".[2]

At nineteen Lightfoot entered Trinity College, Cambridge, and read Classics with Westcott, who had preceded him, and of whose goodness and help he wrote in glowing terms to Benson whom he had left at school at Birmingham.

He took, as Westcott had done, a double first in honours in 1851—both as a Wrangler in Mathematics, and Senior Classic, and first Chancellor's Medallist in

[1] *Salpisei*. A Memorial Sermon (on 1 Cor. xv. 52) preached after the death of J. Prince Lee, first Bishop of Manchester, 2nd Ed., with appendix containing Memorial Notices of the late Bishop by J. F. Wickenden, etc. London, 1870.

[2] "At school the power and diligence of the future theologian were brought into view from time to time. We hear of the boys' astonishment, and their master's delight at indications of his private reading, e.g. in the Fathers, which used to come out incidentally in class." "Joseph Barber Lightfoot," *The Cambridge Review*, Jan. 16th, 1890.

Classics. Next year he was elected Fellow of Trinity, and became a Tutor in 1859. Meanwhile he had been ordained Deacon by his old headmaster in 1854 and Priest four years later. In 1861 he was elected Hulsean Professor of Divinity, but in 1870, when the Regius Professorship fell vacant, he deliberately stood aside, and succeeded in calling his friend Westcott back to Cambridge "to occupy a place" as Westcott testified long afterwards "which was his own by right".

In 1875, however, he became Lady Margaret Professor of Divinity. From his first Professorship in 1861 began a series of lectures on the New Testament, and especially on the Epistles of St Paul, unmatched for brilliance, thoroughness and clearness of exposition, which eventually burst the bounds of the largest lecture rooms in Cambridge and had to be delivered in the great hall of Trinity College, attended by crowds of undergraduates and many other residents of the University.[1] In these years, together with Westcott and Hort, he inspired and fostered a school of Cambridge theology which has not ceased to influence the religious thought of our day, at home and abroad.

Bishop Moule, who was to follow him at Durham, after Bishop Westcott, recalled the days when he was at Cambridge. In an Inaugural Address to the Durham and Northumberland Branch of the Classical Association[2] he said:

[1] "The late Master of Trinity was not given to enthusiasm, but once he did wax enthusiastic as he described the passage between the Senate House and Caius College 'black with the fluttering gowns of students' hurrying to imbibe in the Professor's classroom a knowledge of the New Testament such as was not open to their less happy predecessors." *Contemporary Review*, Feb. 1890, p. 175.

[2] *My Cambridge Classical Teachers*, Feb. 22nd, 1913. Durham: Andrews and Co.

I transport your thoughts backward over some fifty years. It was at Eastertide in 1864 that I took my degree of bachelor. Three years and a half before that date in October 1860, I was entered at Trinity College as Mr Lightfoot's pupil...I found myself the pupil of men, as I realised better afterwards than at the time, who were as vigilant of the sacred letter of Homer or Horace, of Plato or Tacitus, as ever a Bentley or a Porson could be, but who also saw the immortal authors not only as consummate embodiments of a perfect grammar, but as *men* who felt and thought....My college tutor and first college lecturer was Joseph Lightfoot, afterwards, as all men know, Bishop of Durham: mighty master of apostolic and subapostolic literature, strong defender of the faith, shepherd of the people, admirable friend of his friends, illumi-native teacher of his young pupils in those distant Cambridge days.

I came first into his presence when in June 1860 I called on him at his rooms—the rooms which had been Isaac Newton's, nearly two cen-turies before—and asked to be entered on his list of freshmen. Desper-ately shy was I. And he, if I do not mistake, felt a little shy too, for it was his nature so to be. But though a Cambridge Tutor certainly in those days could not possibly be intimate with all his pupils, he exer-cised from the very first a very powerful influence on me by the magnetism of the good greatness of his personality, and the truehearted kindness which looked always through his reserve. All through those years, he was laying the deep foundations of his vast theological know-ledge, chiefly in the vacations, and (during term time) by night. No man ever loitered so late in the Great Court that he did not see Light-foot's lamp burning in his study window, though no man either was so regularly present in morning Chapel at seven o'clock that he did not find Lightfoot always there with him.

But to us he was not the divine but the tutor whom we consulted about our questions and troubles and our admirable lecturer in Herodotus, Euripides and Aeschylus. As later, so then, his strong points were unfailing thoroughness of knowledge and unsurpassable clearness of exposition and instruction. He is said to have written his answers and exercises during the long week of his examination for degree without making one solitary mistake: and I can well believe it. A surer mind never worked. And he had withal quite sympathy enough with our less sure capacities to enable his class to follow him with conviction in every daylight step of his teaching. With many a pleasant touch of humour would he gladden our hearts by the way. I hear him still expounding that curious passage in Herodotus' account of Egypt where he tells us of the Pharaoh who, by isolating new-born babes from sound of speech, endeavoured to discover the primitive language—Lightfoot illustrated this by narrating a similar experiment tried, I think, by the royal wisdom of James I. And the result, so he informed us, in a grave voice all his own, was interesting: "the poor little children spoke pure Hebrew".

For some of his classical pupils, he arranged a private evening lecture in his own rooms. The "Agamemnon" was his theme: the Aeschylean Trilogy, I believe, had long been a special study with him. He spent some time on those occasions over the text as well as the rendering in a way striking and suggestive, working out emendations with great felicity. But I cannot forget how "many lights" in that "upper chamber" did sometimes bring sleep to my eyelids as to those of Eutychus of old. My Aeschylus still shows traces of it, in certain pencil notes of imperfect coherency. But the lights, not the lecturer, were to blame.

At intervals we were asked in groups to dinner in those same historic rooms. We had a cheerful and most friendly host: he seemed much less shy with a large company than when one went to him alone.

He preached sometimes in chapel. The power of voice and force of thought always controlled attention. I remember one noble sermon in which he dwelt on the immortality of our powers, and how the intellect trained aright in this life would be used for God for ever amidst boundless interests in the life to come.

A very different environment in which to watch Lightfoot was the towing-path at the Lent and May races. He often ran with the boats with amazing energy. No doubt he really cared for the race, though I do not think he had ever rowed. But I remember his saying later that he frequented the towing-path not least because "You can get a good run there without being thought a perfect lunatic".

An excellent story belongs to this period, which re-veals Lightfoot's chivalry and lightness of touch in dealing with an erring undergraduate. The culprit tells the story against himself:

I was an active and rather erratic undergraduate of the College. My brother was a great racquet player, and I had arranged to go to London for the day to see him play. The day before I was to go he wrote suggesting that I should dine with him after the match, and stay that night with him in Town. I knew I should not get leave, so I prepared a little plot to cover my transgression. I wrote out this telegram to be sent to my tutor, who happened to be Lightfoot:

"Much regret, have missed the last train am staying with brother".

Arrived at King's Cross in the morning, I gave the telegram to a porter with strict injunctions to send it off *as soon as the last train had started at night*.

On returning to Cambridge next day, I found a message waiting for me from my tutor. This is what happened when I stood before him. He began "Mr Nemo you were not in College last night". "No Sir..." I began, but Lightfoot held up his hand, saying "One moment Mr Nemo, before saying any more please look at this telegram and notice *the hour at which it was sent off*". It had been despatched at *11.45 a.m.*!! The wretched porter, having pocketed his tip, had gone straight off and handed in the telegram at once. Most men would have let me convict myself up to the hilt, but Lightfoot was too great a gentleman. I never can forget it.

Meanwhile Professor Lightfoot had been chosen for other appointments outside the University, being (at different times) Chaplain to the Prince Consort when Chancellor of the University, Chaplain to Queen Victoria, and later Deputy Clerk of the Closet. He was held in very high regard by King Edward VII (when Prince of Wales) whose tutor he had been when the Prince was a member of Trinity College in 1861. He also found time to act as Examining Chaplain to Archbishop Tait at both Fulham and Lambeth, and took such an active and able share in University affairs as to evoke the well-known contrast by a shrewd observer between him and his friend and colleague, that "Westcott ought to have been a mystic of the second century—

and Lightfoot the Chairman of an English Railway Company, and I wish I had shares in it!"

In November 1870 Professor Lightfoot transferred the sum of £4500 to the University to found three University Scholarships for the encouragement of Ecclesiastical History. These are known as the Lightfoot Scholarships. (See Chap. xiv.)

One more great task fell to his lot, to act on the Committee for the Revised Version of the English New Testament. To him a language was an exact expression of the life of a country or a period, and he was one of the first to vindicate the Greek of the New Testament as the genuine *lingua franca* of the Graeco-Roman world of that day, a fact remarkably corroborated since his death by the discovery of the Egyptian papyri. His convictions, published beforehand in a book on the need for such a revision, and still more his insistence, in common with Biblical scholars like Westcott and Moulton and Hort, on the necessity of a thorough examination of the Greek text, and exact and uniform rendering of the words, largely influenced the work of the Revisers. The Revised Version, however, valuable as it is as a more correct rendering of the original Greek, has never become a popular version for the English people.

It is impossible to convey in a few words any idea of the magnitude of Lightfoot's work at Cambridge, as a theologian, a biblical expositor, a historian, or a teacher. It is enough to say of his marvellous output of writings that they arrested the attention of scholars throughout the world, and yet found their way into thousands of homes of clergy and ministers of all denominations.

It was within five years from taking his degree that he first began his work on the Ignatian Epistles, a subject on which he was closely engaged for nearly thirty years, and the results of which were published in his edition of St Ignatius and St Polycarp in June 1885. A second edition of this was already called for in 1888. This great work, which reaches about 1850 pages in three volumes, forms practically a complete repertory of information on the whole history and circumstances of the sub-apostolic age. There is scarcely a point in all the Church life of the first half of the second century that is not dealt with.

As an instance of the extraordinary influence of his learning and authority among scholars may be cited the effect of his remarkable essays published in the *Contemporary Review* between December 1874 and May 1877, in criticism of an anonymous book entitled *Supernatural Religion*. This apparently learned book was a vigorous attack upon the credibility of the Christian Fathers, especially those of the second century. A rumour attributing the authorship of this book to a learned Bishop of the Anglican Church, himself a distinguished historian and scholar, Bishop Thirlwall, together with a chorus of praise from the critics of its scholarship and learning, ensured for it a large circulation, and several editions very quickly appeared. It was vigorously answered by more than one distinguished theologian. But, Lightfoot's articles revealed so many gross mis-statements, that the book quickly lost its importance in the learned world. The Dean of Lichfield, who was closely following the controversy at the time, writes:

I remember a conversation, in the early eighties, with a well-known bookseller about Lightfoot's articles and he told me, in his quiet and judicial way, that they constituted the most remarkable phenomenon in the publishing trade that he had ever known or heard of. "When the book *Supernatural Religion* appeared", he said, "it had an extraordinary reception. It was emphatically praised by the Reviewers, and its sale was so rapid that the publishers could hardly produce it, in its succes- sive editions, fast enough to meet the demand. But before the series of Dr Lightfoot's articles was even approaching completion, the book was already a glut in the second-hand market".

Meanwhile, after declining in 1867 Lord Derby's offer of the See of Lichfield, he was nominated in 1871 by Mr Gladstone to be Canon of St Paul's, and the appoint- ment brought out his great gifts as a preacher. Arch- bishop Tait was once speaking about him to a friend, and said, "He did me the honour of being one of my examining Chaplains, and", he added with some hesi- tation, "we found him—rather heavy. Then he went to St Paul's, where finding himself associated with Canon Liddon, the dullness disappeared, and he became the extraordinarily eloquent preacher that we afterwards knew".

What this intercourse with Liddon meant is well pictured in a pretty scene in the last summer of the Bishop's life. Canon Liddon had come to Auckland to see him, and as he and the Chaplain approached the Castle, they saw the Bishop standing by his open study window. Instantly taking off his hat, Liddon hurried to the window to grasp the hand of his friend.

What the Bishop thought of the Canon is shewn in the dedication of his *Ignatius*:

To Henry Parry Liddon, D.D., to whom God has given special gifts as a Christian Preacher, and matched the gifts with the opportunities, assigning to him his place beneath the great dome of St Paul's, the centre of the world's concourse.

This friendship had great influence on the Church life of the seventies. It was an anxious decade for church- men. The climax was reached when the Archbishop of

Canterbury in April 1874 introduced the Public Worship
Regulation Act, thereby invoking the aid of Parliament
in putting down ritualism by means of prosecutions, and
enforcing a rigid uniformity in the conduct of divine
worship.

One obvious help towards curing the general unrest
was to make the Metropolitan Cathedral a strong centre
of vigorous, consistent and holy Church life. In the
providence of God there came to St Paul's a wonderful
leader in Dean Church, who had weathered the storms
of the Oxford Movement in 1845. Resolute, dauntless
and reserved, he was just the leader needed, and he
found at St Paul's an extraordinary "quaternion of
soldiers".

Canon Scott Holland has described them:[1]

They were alive to all the rising demands which the quickened
Church life must make on a Cathedral: they possessed among them a
brilliant combination of the very gifts which could enable them to
respond to these demands. Already the movement of a new activity
was astir.

Gregory and Liddon were already in action and all their activity was
at the immediate disposal of the new Dean. To them had just been
added Lightfoot, with his unrivalled reputation as a critical scholar, his
glowing ardour of speech, his robust sense of equity, his delightful
geniality. There could never be any difficulty in securing his co-
operation in anything that made for the effective utilisation of the great
Church: and the united force of such a body carried along with it the
kindly courtesy of Bishop Claughton who had just been appointed
Archdeacon.

Thus the Dean found himself in the rare position of heading a
Chapter which was ready to act with practical unanimity. It was a
corporate body that was animated by a single purpose....It was to this
unity of purpose and mind that Dr Liddon continually attributed all
that the Chapter succeeded in achieving at St Paul's.

[1] *Dean Church's Life and Letters*, pp. 214 etc.

During his residence, Canon Lightfoot gathered round him young men to whom he specially devoted himself.

The possibility of breaking up such a combination by losing Canon Lightfoot was overwhelming to the Dean. He pleaded hard that he should not go to Durham, he was far too valuable at St Paul's. He writes to Bishop Benson of Truro:

DEANERY, ST PAUL'S.
January 23rd, 1879.

My dear Bishop of Truro,

...This most anxious matter touches us both so deeply, and not us only but greater things. The thought of losing him is dreadful....All you urge is of the greatest weight....It is the point the Archbishop urged when Lightfoot saw him yesterday,—and with good reason—though he frightened Lightfoot by expressing anxiety as to who there would be to take *his own place* if he were removed....And I am worldly enough too—to feel a great rising of heart at the recognition, with such, and not inadequate, honour of the first scholar of the English Church. But yet even for that I do look with distress at the breaking off just now of the career he has deliberately designed for himself which he is filling so nobly and usefully and in which he leaves no successor, none I mean of the same rare and commanding powers. For he is not only full of knowledge, he is able to make knowledge *live*. He is able to animate it with the sense of its connection with the needs and hopes of present modern life....

I do not know how he will decide; to-morrow I suppose he will settle. He is still torn and perplexed. But if he goes to Durham, Bishop Butler will have a successor worthy of him in the combination of innocence, simplicity and pure nobleness of thought and purpose with intellectual forces which make his fellows wonder and admire.

But oh dear! if he leaves St Paul's...

Ever yours affectionately
R. W. CHURCH[1]

The great Dean's fears were more than dispelled. In 1884, writing to Canon Stubbs, Lightfoot's successor at

---

[1] *Dean Church's Life and Letters*, pp. 271–3.

St Paul's, who was hesitating to accept the Bishopric of Chester, Dean Church wrote:

> I do so deeply sympathise with you in your trial....But Lightfoot's sacrifice is a great encouragement. He would not be so nobly happy as he is now, if he had—as I wished him—shrunk from the call.[1]

That happiness is well described by Bishop Moule, viewing the great scholar's episcopate from the vantage ground of the same throne, eighteen years later, and thence reverting once more to Cambridge days.

In his "Commemoration Sermon"[2] at Trinity College, Cambridge, in 1907 he said:

> ...How shall I discourse as I would of Joseph Lightfoot?
>
> Before me now in the daily path of duty and intercourse, his name is always moving as a great and living force. First in time of the two mighty men of God, who successively occupied of later years the Chair of Durham, and who made between them a continuity of combined mental and spiritual greatness to which it is difficult to find a parallel, Lightfoot still retains in the hearts of both clergy and people a place not of honour only, but of love with which not even the splendour of Westcott's venerated and more recent memory interferes. "Dear Bishop Lightfoot" is his common designation in the faithful-hearted North; and men recall his grand humanity, with its gladness and its tears, even more vividly than his immense knowledge, his masterly administration, his supreme sanity of judgment, and his literally life-breaking toil. Then behind his great episcopate lie the times of his epoch-making activity as student and teacher at Cambridge and St Paul's. Within those years from 1861 to 1879, step by step, work by work, as expositor, historian, as consummate defender of the historic faith, he grew to be a power for good in Christian minds and souls, unsurpassed if not unrivalled for its magnificent wholeness and soundness of result.
>
> In a leading article issued just after his death, *The Times* paid a noble tribute to the astonishing achievement of his literary labours in giving a

[1] *Letters of William Stubbs, Bishop of Chester*, p. 253.
[2] *Wise Men and Scribes* is the Title of the "Commemoration Sermon", 1907.

new trend of thought, a trend towards faith, over vast regions of the educated world. The panegyric, for such it is throughout without reserve, dwells upon "the noble character and splendid faculties", which somehow, and not least I think, by his perfect combination of wisdom with knowledge, and of modesty with authoritative power, so found response in the public estimate that (in the words of the writer of the article) "his virtues were never doubted, his mental eminence depreciated, or the appropriate rewards withheld".

But to-night I speak of Lightfoot less as the great Bishop and great Professor than as the Fellow and Tutor of this College, under whom it was my happiness to enter seven and forty years ago.

Only for one year did we enjoy his guidance for in 1861 he succeeded to the Hulsean Chair: but that short year laid an influence for life upon mind and aims. And how did the influence operate? By no means in any overt and elaborate fashion. To all but an intimate few of our time Lightfoot was reserved in individual intercourse....

His sermons happily not infrequent were always uplifting by their strength of reason, their freshness of insight and application, and an eloquence only less of form than of soul. But his power upon us was mainly and continuously exercised through the manifestation of what he was. To watch his simple but profound devotion day by day in this Chapel, to see a little of his splendid diligence in toil and duty...to know by a sure instinct, as we talked about him, or heard rumours of him, that he was always and everywhere the same, the Christian man using very great gifts wholly for God and for others: all this meant for us a perpetual moral impression of the sort to tell, just at our time of life, for the purest and most lasting good.[1] Well may his memory by us be blessed for ever.

We could not possibly at that period know anything in detail of the secret inspiration which made such a life possible....But I have come since to know a little of his sources of patience and of power, and how

[1] "His lectures on the Greek Testament were distinguished not only by their ability, but also by their spiritual power. A pupil who attended one of the earliest courses remarks: 'I remember well how much the class was impressed when, after giving us the usual introductory matter Lightfoot closed the book and said, "After all said and done, the only way to know the Greek Testament properly is by prayer", and dwelt further on this thought'." "Joseph Barber Lightfoot," *The Cambridge Review*, Jan. 16th and 23rd, 1890.

they were hidden with Christ in God. His near friend of the latest years, Dr Watkins, Canon and Archdeacon of Durham, possesses an engraving of Dürer's "Crucifixion" which always hung beside Light-foot's simple bedstead at Auckland, brought, I believe, from his Cambridge rooms. Below the picture runs the legend "ES IST VOLLBRACHT", the "It is Finished" of the Crucified. To my dear Tutor, deep within the heart of his most noble life, the Incarnate Christ of Atonement and Resurrection was all in all—salvation, desire, motive, resource, life, way and end. The magnetism of his influence upon us rose ultimately, behind all the massive complex of gifts and acquirements, from *him* who dwelt in his heart by faith.

The Dean of Durham (Bishop Welldon) writes:

How well I remember his farewell sermon in St Mary's Church, before he left Cambridge for Durham. As I walked to the Church I saw him coming to the Vestry with his bag containing his robes in his hand. The University Church was packed to the doors. There was something in the scene which moved me almost to tears, so strongly did I realise what had been the value of his influence in the University, and what would be the loss, when he would be no more seen or heard except at rare intervals in Cambridge.

I came to stay with him at Auckland Castle soon after his consecra-tion.

When I think of his recluse life at Cambridge, it is an astonishment to know how in both Durham and Northumberland he won his way to the confidence and affection, not only of the Clergy, but of the mine-owners and miners, the leaders of industry and territorial magnates.

Never before has there been a more splendid combination of learning, wisdom, and piety than in Bishop Lightfoot. I can only add as one who lives in the Diocese over which he presided for ten years—that every year I spend in it increases my admiration for his episcopate.

Chapter II

CONSECRATION AS BISHOP

WHEN it was announced on January 28th, 1879, that Professor Lightfoot had been appointed Bishop of Durham, the news was hailed with joy everywhere. Archbishop Tait wrote: "Lightfoot's appointment to Durham opens a bright prospect, a man of really humble mind, of great learning, and perfect scholarship—his influence will be like Cotton's in India".[1]

Acting as he always did on Prince Lee's motto, "Virtus in agendo constat", the new Bishop had within a week chosen and appointed his two first domestic Chaplains—H. E. Savage (now Dean of Lichfield), then a resident Fellow of Corpus Christi College, Cambridge, and G. R. Eden (afterwards Bishop of Wakefield), a Master at the time at Aysgarth Preparatory School.

On Easter Tuesday, April 15th, he paid his first visit to Auckland with these Chaplains. A thorough inspection was made of the Castle and Park, and plans were discussed, which were already clear in that far-seeing mind.

On passing the fine Gatehouse at the entrance to the Park from the market-place, the Bishop—who had lived all his life alone in College rooms and dreaded the idea of a domestic establishment—looked up and said with genuine feeling, "Ah if they would only let you and me

[1] *Life of Archbishop Tait*, II, 517.

live there ". Little did any of the three realise how wonderfully the old promise would be fulfilled, "God setteth the
solitary in families ". Truly those rambling corridors and
great rooms in the historic castle held for ten years a
unique family around the "solitary man", himself perhaps the happiest of the circle of devoted "sons" and
servants.

Four days later Eden found himself installed as secretary
in Lightfoot's rooms at Trinity, Cambridge, Savage
joining them daily from Corpus. One of Lightfoot's
rare traits was the leaving of important correspondence
to his subordinates when once he had learned to trust
them, without afterwards looking at what they had
written. He was a believer in Jethro's advice to Moses,
and by freely delegating work to others he left his mind
free for great problems and deep study.

On April 23rd, St George's Day, taking Eden with
him he left Cambridge for his Consecration in Westminster Abbey. They stayed at his usual home in London, in St Paul's Chapter House, a brick building on
the north side of the Cathedral, now occupied by Lloyds
Bank. Here he had lived in simple style during his
residence, almost like life in college, with a housekeeper
who might have been a Cambridge bedmaker.

Next day Dean Church and all the Canons specially
attended Evensong with their colleague for the last time.
And at nine o'clock that evening Dr Westcott conducted
a quiet informal service of prayer for an inner circle of
friends in preparation for the morrow.

St Mark's Day broke fine and glorious, with all the
hope of spring even in London.

Considerable surprise was felt that the Consecration
was held in the Southern Province (for which there

was no precedent since the Consecration of the great Bishop Cosin), and that it was not in St Paul's, with which Dr Lightfoot was connected, which would have held the hosts of Cambridge and other friends who wished to be present. It was not in St Paul's because the Northern Primate did not wish to intrude into the domain of the Archbishop of Canterbury. But the space available in the Abbey was far too small to admit all who came.

The usual protest was made by the Dean and Chapter, Westminster Abbey being a "Royal Peculiar"; the Dean stated that he granted permission in pursuance of a Mandate from the Queen.

The Archbishop of York was accompanied by the Bishops of Carlisle, Manchester, Sodor and Man from the Northern, and the Bishops of London, Winchester, Ely and Truro from the Southern Province.

The procession from the Jerusalem Chamber included the whole Chapter of Westminster, the Master and Fellows of Trinity, and the Members of the Revision Committee of the New Testament, and it made its way through serried ranks of clergy in their black gowns.

The Bishops of London and Ely, his former Diocesans, presented the new Bishop. The sermon was by his lifelong friend Dr Westcott, and the offertory was for the Endowment of the new See of Newcastle.

Dr Westcott's sermon was remarkable for its concentrated power. Choosing as his text "From strength to strength" (Psa. lxxxiv. 7), he began by pointing out that this psalm is the Hymn of Divine Life in all ages.[1] "It brings before us the grace and glory of sacrifice, of service, of progress, where God alone, the Lord of hosts,

[1] *From Strength to Strength*, Three Sermons, Macmillan, 1890.

is the source and the strength, and the end of effort." The lesson of the past was all summed up in the phrase "from strength to strength". In illustration he gave a rapid sketch of the whole history of "the great Northum⁄brian Diocese . . . a chequered life, grievously troubled by passion, yet continuous with a mighty power, and un⁄broken by revolutions. The saint, the scholar, the soldier, the courtier, the statesman, the divine, have added some⁄thing to the episcopal inheritance of the See of Aldhun".

While the glorious past was thus present in imagination, the unknown future was represented in person to carry on the tale. Hidden in the Organ loft, unseen by the preacher, there sat a schoolboy, an interested listener, who became one of Bishop Lightfoot's examining Chaplains, and is one of England's ablest Bishops to⁄day.

The Bishop spent the evening of that memorable day at the Chapter House of St Paul's with his Chaplains.

Next day he returned to Cambridge. He was feeling deeply the severance from St Paul's, and all its associa⁄tions, and its goodly fellowship. But that parting was relieved by an incident which greatly amused him. The good caretaker, swelling with pride at her master's new dignity, when all was ready for departure, threw open the dining room door with a new air, and announced in loud voice, "Your carriage is at the door, my Lord". The Bishop went to the window, and vainly trying to conceal his laughter, called his Chaplain to see "the Bishop's carriage". There in pouring rain stood one of the dirtiest and most dilapidated of London "growlers", with a driver to match, a sack on his shoulders, and a pipe upside down in his mouth! It was a good story to tell the dignified Bishop Benson of Truro (the University

preacher of next day) who travelled with them to
Cambridge.

Thus began the Golden Age of Durham. The Bishop
started with a light heart, because of his strong confidence.
He had written on January 27th to Professor Westcott:

At length I have sent my answer "Yes". It seemed to me that to
resist any longer would be θεομαχεῖν [to fight against God]. My con-
solation and my hope for the future is that it has cost me the greatest
moral effort, the greatest venture of faith which I ever made. Now that
the answer is sent I intend to have no regrets about the past.

AT AUCKLAND CASTLE

"In the strangely altered circumstances of our time, much, very much, has changed, and mainly, I fear, not for the better; but one thing is unchanged and unchangeable, viz. *the affectionate homage which invests the name of Bishop Lightfoot.*"

BISHOP OF DURHAM

(Letter inviting "Sons of the House" to Auckland Castle for St Peter's Day, 1926)

Chapter III

SONS OF THE HOUSE

ONE day as he was strolling across the quadrangle at Keble College, Oxford, in the early summer of 1879, young F. W. Glyn was accosted by the Warden, Dr Talbot (afterwards Bishop of Winchester), with the question "Would you like to go to Auckland Castle?" "Where in the world is that?" was his reply. "Where the Bishop of Durham lives", said the Warden, "he has asked me to pick out some young men from Oxford to go, as the first of a series of men, to be trained for Holy Orders under the Bishop's own eye."

The invitation was accepted, and thus the Auckland family began.

Fred Glyn came to the Castle at Michaelmas 1879 to join Fred Eden and Fred Cope, both from Pembroke College, Cambridge; and these under the Rev. George Eden and the Rev. H. E. Savage became Bishop Lightfoot's "three mighty men" who started the Brotherhood that has had such potent influence in Durham Diocese and beyond.

The following letters give a glimpse of early days at the Castle, and reveal the Bishop's affection towards his young men.

To the Warden of Keble.
AUCKLAND CASTLE,
BISHOP AUCKLAND.
November 10th, 1879.

My dear Warden,

I am not sitting down to write a formal letter, but I thought you would be glad to know what satisfaction I have in Glyn in all ways.

I find him a most pleasant inmate of my house and he is taking very kindly to his work both practical and intellectual. His fellow-students and he are already most excellent friends and altogether we are a very happy household.

I have been much away hitherto with Confirmation and other work, but hope to see more of them now. Any other Keble man like Glyn whom you recommend will be welcome here so long as I have a place for him and indeed I would endeavour to make a place. Of all his fellow-students I can speak in the highest terms.

Very sincerely yours,

J. B. DUNELM.

The Lightfoot generation was necessarily unique. We were received as "Sons of the House" in a way only possible to a Bishop who was unmarried, and had no lady to preside over the domestic arrangements of Auckland Castle.

Bishop Westcott, who was married, naturally could not do this and provided other arrangements, billeting the students in the house at the lodge gates with a Chaplain as Dean. This system was carried on more or less on the same lines by Bishop Moule. Thus in the later generations the intercourse, though much closer than at a Theological College, was necessarily not on the same intimate footing.

This was partly shewn by the fact that as time went on, at the annual St Peter's Day Reunion of the Brotherhood, the proportion of Lightfoot men was always greater than that of those who came subsequently. Yet the senior men, in the spirit of Lightfoot's own wonderful sympathy, never allowed any distinction to appear, or to be felt between different generations of students. And the same spirit even now animates our triennial meetings, though the senior men may be in age rather fathers than brothers to some of the younger generation.

In Bishop Westcott's day the Castle lunch was the students' midday dinner, when all gathered round the Bishop's table. But we shared every meal and every Chapel service with Bishop Lightfoot.

The value of this close intercourse with such a man was incalculable. One lesson at least it taught us. He was, as he had always been, a tremendous worker, and we caught something of his enthusiasm for work. Auckland Castle was a busy and punctual house. Even during his early breakfast with us the Bishop would be opening and piling up his very numerous letters, with his waste-paper basket at his side for the envelopes. Then he would glance through the newspaper, especially the late Mr Joseph Cowen's clever London Letter in the *Newcastle Chronicle*.

After breakfast we went to the Chapel, where Bishop, Chaplains and choir boys robed. We said shortened Morning Prayer, with a hymn, the Bishop reading the Lesson from the Revised Version. Then all separated, going to our several bedrooms where we read by ourselves, except when we attended lectures.

After luncheon each of us visited his own district— Bishop Auckland is the centre of a Decapolis of Pit villages and the two Vicars placed a student in one or other to help the six curates and to learn parish work.

Their experiences can best be told by two extracts.

The Bishop wrote a long obituary to *Chanticleer* (Lent term 1887), the Jesus College, Cambridge, magazine, in memory of H. R. Banton, who had been a student and later became his Chaplain. In sending the notice the Bishop wrote: "I am glad of the opportunity which you have given me of paying this tribute to the memory of one whom I loved as a son".

After reviewing his earlier life the Bishop proceeds:

The students at Auckland Castle are told off to different departments of parochial work and Banton was placed in St Peter's Parish in the Mission Room District which was largely inhabited at that time by iron workers, a very rough and unmanageable class of men. The Rev. F. L. Cope who had himself been an Auckland student was then curate of the parish. They had known each other at Cambridge, and from notes with which at my request he supplied me I extract the following: "At Auckland I notice the beginning of his distinctive method of working: i.e. fastening himself on one or two at a time and paying much attention to them. It is difficult to say what guided him in his choice. Often they were to me the most unattractive and unpromising specimens."

The Bishop continues:

Knowing his innate sensitiveness and refinement, I can only suppose him to have acted in the spirit of St Francis of Assisi, lavishing his attentions on those who would otherwise receive scant attention, and feeling at the same time that his own fastidious taste needed the stern discipline of such companionships.

Another vivid picture is given by Arthur F. Sim, the Trial Eight stroke of Pembroke College, Cambridge, of whom the Bishop said at his ordination: "There are depths in Sim that I cannot fathom". "Let him go where he will, his face will be a sermon in itself." In one of his letters Sim gives this sketch of the life at Auckland Castle:

One has an indefinite amount of work to do, so I will give you a sample of the way we spend the day. Breakfast at 7.45—Chapel 8.15. Lectures 9 to 11—Reading 11 to 1—Lunch at 1.15. Then in the afternoon we visit three times a week and read the other three days. I generally get a game, and sometimes two, of football in the week by way of exercise. My district is a sort of cosmopolitan one. I visit the parents of the institute lads. The institute was built by the Bishop and it is a sort of club for young men and lads from 18 years upwards. There are about 200 in it, so there is lots to do and I am teaching one of them to read, a slow process! I have a Bible Class on Sunday and I read the Lessons in the Parish Church.

Occasionally I have to preach in a schoolroom some three miles out in the country, but more often in a tiny little room in the town, where my congregation consists of about four to twelve old women and a lot of children. The latter are never quiet, and to have one of them squalling in one's ear is rather disconcerting, though not to the mothers who are accustomed to it.

After Curacies at Sunderland and West Hartlepool Sim volunteered for work in Central Africa under U.M.C.A. Before he went, one of us said: "Peter, it's a terrible sacrifice going to Africa, giving up all the comforts, leaving all the friends and facing an almost certain death". He was silent for a minute looking out of the window. Then he said quietly: "He's worth it all, Mac." All his life long he seemed to have been looking up into the face of God. That was, we felt, what made his face so beautiful.

One day at Sunderland he jumped straight into the river and saved a drowning boy. His fellow Curate living in the same house contradicted the rumour when he heard it, but found later it was true, though Peter in his modesty had never even mentioned it to him. When the Bishop knew he wrote from his sick bed:

BOURNEMOUTH.

March /89.

My dear Sim,

I have heard with very great delight that you have rescued a child from drowning, a special privilege on which I congratulate you as one of my Auckland sons. We all feel that the honour is reflected on the whole body, and we thank you for the lift you have given us.

As yet I have only heard the fact. Write and tell me the particulars.

I hope you will be able to come and pay me a visit here, though you will find a sick man a very dull host. But you will find livelier companions. However Harmer will shortly write about this.

This is one of the very few letters which I have written since I took up the pen, after five months: and both pen and brain play me sad pranks. But I desired to express my thanks to you with my own hand.

Yours affectionately,

J. B. DUNELM.

Most affectionate remembrances to Willink, Lambert, Rolt, and all my Auckland sons.

The original of this precious letter, which had some "sad pranks" corrected by the Bishop himself, was taken out by Sim as a treasure to Kota Kota where he died after ten days' weary suffering on October 29th, 1895.

This Arthur F. Sim—"Peter Sim"—is still one of the inspirations of Auckland Brethren; as Canon Body said after his death "he is to me no memory but a felt presence still".

In 1884 the learned world was aroused by the discovery by Bryennios of the "Didache": and on St Peter's Day, when he had all his sons about him, the Bishop discussed the new discovery. We all sat in the great drawing-room and the Bishop stood, or sat, at a spot near the great door towards the Chapel, and gave a most learned and vigorous lecture on the subject in the most outspoken way.[1]

But while thus ready to open all his mind to his own sons it was otherwise with strangers.

That same summer a learned foreign historian came to luncheon. Two ladies, cousins of the Bishop, were staying at the Castle and there was a large party. The Bishop took in one lady and the learned stranger sat opposite beside

[1] See *Apostolic Fathers*, Single vol. pp. 215 etc.

the other. Having engineered his conversation with her round to the Didache, he suddenly raised his voice, as he told her his views of the meaning of a debatable passage, adding, "Don't you think so, my Lord?" across the table.

We Chaplains and students watched with some amuse- ment. We knew that the Bishop was not to be drawn. He seemed to ignore the question. Luncheon was the immediate business in hand, and his guests must not be delayed; so the learned stranger found that though his own opinion was listened to with courtesy his question received no reply. His Chaplain said to the Bishop afterwards, "You didn't give him much satisfaction". His only answer was "I couldn't think what he was talking about; he called it the Titt-a-hay!"

A still better example of the same rooted objection to being forced to give an opinion prematurely on any question occurred when a certain very well-known pub- licist asked if he might introduce a prominent newspaper editor. The Bishop's hospitality welcomed them and they came, clearly agreed between themselves to extract an opinion from the Bishop on a very crucial ecclesiastical issue then causing great anxiety in Church circles. We watched with interest at luncheon as the Bishop skilfully parried their many leading questions. Now and then when escape seemed impossible, quite suddenly he would turn the conversation.

In despair as they rose from the table the two strangers followed the Bishop to the window; when one of them pressed his point, and said, "And what, my Lord, do you think of the prospect?" the Bishop put up his eye- glass, and looking out said with grave simplicity, "I always say that it is one of the advantages of my house that though it is in the town, it is also in the country. It is a wonderful prospect".

"It was difficult", says one of his sons, "for a shy man awed by the Bishop's learning to come into close relation-ship with him. Yet one felt how much he sought the affection of those around him: seeking it that they might share his larger love.

All this led the Bishop to take walks with his men, sometimes long walks with a number of students and chaplains, including a railway journey. Another day he would go with one Chaplain or a student to Parkhead, or to Binchester, the old Roman camp a mile or two from the head of the Park, taking his big Saint Bernard dog whose reckless career he delighted in, regardless of what it cost in compensation for sheep. At Brancepeth he would discuss the dates and history of its treasures with his wide and accurate knowledge. These excursions gave opportunity for love to grow, and for him to know the character of his men.

One veteran writes after the lapse of forty years:

The event that sticks in my mind above all else was the great kind-ness of our father in God, giving up a whole afternoon's walk with me alone, so that he might hear of a matter in my mind, and advise and talk to me about it. I was generally terribly shy with him, but that time I could not be, he was so understanding and sympathetic. What a lot one learned from his personality!

Sunday night supper was a great occasion, when the local clergy as well as all students were gathered, and the tension of a busy Sunday found relaxation in the merry talk. On one occasion a student who had been preaching at a distant Mission came in late. He was met by the Bishop who, with mock anxiety and eyeglass upraised, said quickly, "How is Eutychus?"

But there came times of a different order, when amid fewer listeners perhaps the Bishop would linger over dinner talking more freely of days and persons of the past. The smaller the company the better the chance of this.

He took the liveliest interest in all his Sons' athletics. It was his custom to lecture on Saturday mornings, but one day finding out that one of us was playing football for the Town he said, "No lecture to-day, so that you can play football".

Another came north with an All England reputation and was in great demand all over the county for football, and the Bishop encouraged his playing. It fell on a day that he landed at a distant station and found no way of getting home, so presuming on the Bishop's kindness he dared to telegraph for the Bishop's dogcart, which was duly sent. Next week the same thing occurred. On the telegram being shown to the Bishop he said quietly, "Send the carriage". When the sportsman turned out of the train he was astonished to see the Bishop's footman in livery waiting, and still more surprised when he found himself taken home in state in the Bishop's carriage and pair. It did not occur again.

The Bishop greatly enjoyed a visit paid to the Castle by Dr Farmer, the well known organist of Harrow School, when he came to conduct a performance of his Oratorio, "Christ and his Soldiers", in the Town Hall. Dr Farmer was a sparkling conversationalist, and in the drawing room gave a humorous musical sketch of his own after the manner of Corney Grain which delighted the Bishop. Indeed he would always break away from his work when a more than usually attractive visitor was speaking to the students; such as the late Dr Dickinson, Dean of the Chapel Royal, Dublin, one of the wittiest of the sons of men. A clever musician, one of the brethren, writes:

In the last summer of his life when Mr Richmond was at the Castle painting his portrait, Richmond and I used to play duets on the great Broadwood Grand Piano in the evenings, chiefly Beethoven's sym/ phonies. But the Bishop's taste in music was not classical, and the one thing he really appreciated was when I did an imitation of a street piano/organ playing "Dreamland Faces", a performance which he insisted on my giving before an audience of many of the grandees of the county, after a big full dress dinner party.

But the same writer has a more precious memory. "My most vivid remembrance of him is just before he went on his last journey to Bournemouth, when each of us went into his study to say 'Good/bye', and I well remember kneeling down, as he gave me his blessing."

And here is another letter that may well close our sketch of life at Auckland:

My dear...

Your letter was a great joy and comfort to me. I trust the sense of Brotherhood will grow ever stronger and stronger with you all as the years roll on. God has given us an ideal, which we ought to cherish as a very sacred possession.

It is always a delight to me to hear that my sons are even happier in the ministerial work than they were at Auckland. This is just what I pray for. I trust that they may carry away a something which by God's goodness may be an abiding source of happiness.

You have been much in my thought lately. Your goodness in looking after me at Oban has often been present to my mind. I do not suppose you can realise how a father lives on the loyalty and attention of his sons.

Always my own dear son,

Yours affectionately,

J. B. DUNELM.

Such was his treatment of his "Sons of the House". And here is his review of his scheme;—

Preaching to us on St Peter's Day, 1889—which proved to be his last—he said:

...In that long wakeful night when the decision was finally made which transferred me from Cambridge to Durham the idea of the College first took shape in my brain. It was thus identified with the work of my episcopate in its origin. It has proved by God's grace, a very real blessing to myself (may I say to ourselves?) and, what is far more important, to this Diocese. It rests with you now that henceforward the promise of the future shall outstrip the achievements of the past.

The idea was not long delayed in the execution. From the commencement of the October Term after my arrival in the Diocese the College dates its birth. Like much greater institutions, its growth has been only the healthier because it arose from small beginnings. It is a great happiness to note that in to-day's meeting we miss none of those who were present at its inauguration.... For two or three years our numbers were so few that a periodical gathering did not enter into our thoughts.

At length on St Peter's Day, 1883, our first Commemoration took place. From that day forward we have had these joyful gatherings annually. [1]

But while thus treating us as his sons, he would have us no esoteric club.

Whatever other affinities may have drawn man to man during their residence here...the true and ultimate bond of union must be the participation in a common work and the loving devotion to a common Master. This is the consecration and the crown of your friendships, of your brotherhood.

Of your brotherhood. Yes, I delight to place this before you as the ideal of our fellowship here. A brotherhood in Christ; not an exclusive association of clique or caste; not a repulsive Pharisaism which exalts special advantages into special merits; not a centripetal, but a centrifugal influence—or rather centrifugal because it is centripetal, a force gathering strength at a central fire, but a force diffusing heat, and light and life far and wide.

... The affection of brother to brother is only a stepping-stone to that larger grace which knows no distinction of man and man which transcends all external barriers.... If it stops short of this it fails of its

[1] *Ordination Addresses*, pp. 196, 197. London: Macmillan, 1890.

true end. It becomes a snare to ourselves, and a stone of offence to the Church of Christ. Remember therefore the Apostle's precept ἐπι-χορηγήσατε ἐν τῇ φιλαδελφίᾳ τὴν ἀγάπην. Let your φιλα-δελφία expand into ἀγάπη.[1]

"He sought our love that he might pass on his love through us to others", writes one "Son". And assuredly love spread among all ranks of his clergy. "Though not a 'Son of the House' I feel surely that I was a 'first Cousin'. His gentleness and sympathy inspired our affection."

But if as Sons we had these "special advantages" we were not to expect any special favours:

I am ambitious for you all. But my ambition does not take the form of wishing to see you in places of emolument or of ease or of comfort or of popularity. I desire before all things that you should be fit to do Christ's work, that you should be ready to do it, and that you should have the scope and opportunity for doing it. I covet for you not the honour of men, but the honour of GOD. If the alternative lay before me of offering any of you a place of emolument and dignity on the one hand, or a place of difficulty and responsibility on the other, be assured that the emolument and the dignity should go elsewhere, and the difficulty and responsibility should be laid on your shoulders, if only I thought them strong enough to bear the burden. I should feel, you would feel (would you not?) that only too much honour was done to you, when you were called to bear the brunt of the fight in the van of God's army, even though your shoulders might wear no epaulettes and you yourselves received less than a subaltern's pay. This—neither more nor less than this—is the meaning of Christ's prediction to St Peter as applied to yourselves. "Expect toil; expect to spend and be spent, expect in some form or other a cross—but in spite of this, or rather because of this, 'Follow ME, Follow ME'."[2]

[1] *Ordination Addresses*, p. 154.
[2] *Ibidem*, p. 160.

Chapter IV

A STRANGER'S IMPRESSIONS

THE following letters give an interesting picture of the home-life at Auckland Castle, seen through the eyes of an observant visitor. The writer, the Rev. Robert W. Barbour of Bonskeid, near Pitlochry, was one of the most gifted of a brilliant circle of Free Church Ministers and Laymen in Scotland at that time. Bishop Lightfoot had spent a memorable four weeks' holiday in the late summer of 1880 at the picturesque Killiecrankie Cottage hard by Bonskeid, and had been greatly charmed by the kindness and hospitality of the Barbour family. Feelings of friendship sprang up out of this visit, and especially so between young Robert Barbour and the Bishop's Chaplain, now Bishop Eden. Hence Robert Barbour's visit to Auckland in 1882, so beautifully described in these letters to his wife.

Robert Barbour's death only nine years later at the age of thirty-six deprived his Church of one who was already recognised as likely to be a leader of outstanding ability and most loveable personality. Scholar, poet, philosopher, pastor, saint—it is hard to say where he most excelled. The letters are reprinted from a privately published *Memoir* (Glasgow University Press, 1893) by the kind permission of his son, Dr G. Freeland Barbour, of Fincastle, Perthshire.

AUCKLAND CASTLE,
April 28th, 1882.

I suppose it is the curfew which has just rung, for my watch says 8 o'clock, and I feel as if I were at home, and indeed should be quite content were my wife and wee one only with me. For I think every true Bethel—every house of God, or of a godly man—feels like home, however different the outward form of the life be. And, indeed, the form here seems to me quite a secondary thing, and quite separable from the reality. The stone and lime of it is different to ours—the choir-stalls and the palace-chapel—but the songs are the same, and the hearts are one. So I felt at the practising to-night. But to say so is to run on to the end of my story. . . .

Why should I tell thee of the walk down the "long, unlovely street" [of Bishop Auckland], the escape from the square through the archway to the great Castle, with its square masses and little ornament, except where the chapel takes hold of the heavy Tudor and lifts it heavenward—not a bad likeness in stone of the Bishop himself? Why should I tell thee what thou knowest? It was good to have been here with thee, it felt safe ground and hardly strange. The absence of any lady was another appropriate element in the experience. One does not know what kind of creature could have sat by the Bishop's side and not have seemed inappropriate, or detracting, or unworthy in some way.

A cup of tea waited in the small drawing-room. . . .

Then we joined the little party in the Chapel. Some six little boys on either side sat in the stalls, Eden just beyond at the harmonium, the men in residence in the back seats. This happens, not every day, but every second, when the psalms and hymns for morning and evening prayers are gone over. . . . The singing was sweet and real, though we were a little rough. I forgot to say that the Bishop had come in while we were having tea. He received me so warmly, and trotted out and in so simply. There is an air almost of wistfulness, a dumb kind of devotion in his face, that gives you an impression of the most downright honesty. You know the way a Newfoundland or a setter looks at you when it wants to show you it loves you. Well, it is not unlike that. I think the cherub with the face of an ox which Ezekiel saw cannot have been far from the Bishop's. Just as Mozley or Westcott make one think of the one with the eagle, and Rainy or J. H. Wilson of the lion, and Livingstone or Dr Stewart or Mr Stalker of the *man*. After chapel we went into the tea-room, Dr Lightfoot showing the way with such a womanly grace. The table was ample, and the table talk easy to a degree. The talk was about the book *John Inglesant*, which everybody had been reading but myself. The Bishop's words were always worth taking to-day. Such a *judgment* it is. He always speaks with a pair of balances in his hand, like Justice, only he is not blindfolded like her. And yet he looks about after speaking like a child, as if to see whether he has not made a mistake. "I know the plot", said one man. "There is plenty of plotting in it, but little plot", rejoined the Bishop, evidently without any sense that he was using the language of repartee. "A curious condition of mind to be in," he went on to remark, "to be scrupulous about honour and to have no regard for the truth." He spoke, too, of the contrast between the contented life of a country gentleman and these sudden stirrings of spirit which came to John Inglesant. "I wonder", he asked, "whether such a state of mind ever existed to any extent in those days." I thought of saying that it was a common enough type of character in our own day, and that the writer had probably carried it thither out of his own time. "But", added Dr Lightfoot, "I imagine the description of Roman Society is perfectly correct." Somebody quoted a lecture of Seeley's on Pope Leo the Atheist *versus* Luther the Dogmatist. "That is putting it very strongly," rejoined the Bishop, "Leo was a sceptic rather." These are just a few crumbs. Meantime, remarks on tennis, offers and acceptances of "grilled chicken", "cocoa", "toast", and college stories flew about. It was not brilliant, but it was very bright. Dr Lightfoot asked after Cults and Pitlochry, and smiled upon us all.

·   ·   ·   ·   ·   ·

10.45. The evening worship was very uniting. The servants came in, and we sang the psalms and hymns, and Dr Lightfoot and a chaplain read and prayed (from the new version and the prayer book) in his own voice and with his own devout, simple soul uttering itself in all. His after talk in the drawing-room was even more charming. You know how a mastiff will lie down (out of sheer love for the canine race) and let a crowd of small dogs jump and tumble over him, and put them off, and egg them on with great pawings and immense "laps" of his broad tongue. Even so did Dr Lightfoot.

Since then Eden and some of the men have come in from the Boys' Institute, where they have spent the evening attempting to solve the impossible—how to command the wild, wicked young life of Bishop Auckland.

It is good for me to be in the midst of so much informal earnestness and Christian manliness.

AUCKLAND CASTLE, BISHOP AUCKLAND,
April 29th, 1882.

I write at an open window of the little drawing-room here. I have so often longed you could have moved about with me through these rooms and among these men; for it is, I think, altogether the best glimpse you can get of the English Church both outside and in. Everything that adds honour to her name is here. There is a good tradition in the Diocese. The Bishops have not seldom been men of piety and power. Butler's memory alone is enough to ennoble any place in any Church; and the history of Auckland Castle both before and after his time is not out of sympathy with the thoughts you have when you hear his name. They are thoughts, are they not, of honest bravery in theology, of a great man doing battle by himself in a quiet corner, until the Church at length awoke and found he had won her victory.

Then I suppose it is not taking her past out of the hands of time, to say that Butler's seat is now filled by his nearest successor; a man as great in his work and in his day as his great namesake (for they both are written "Joseph Dunelm.") I know not if there be any better test of true lastingness in any man who is yet living, than when, knowing his written works, one is able to compare them with his person, and to say that these correspond. The same judgment which you admire in Dr Lightfoot's commentaries meets you in his conversation. He seems, like Justice in her statues, always to give his sentences, holding meantime a pair of other scales. Indeed, the analogy might be extended. Justice is but badly described in stone as being blindfolded in her decisions. But there is in the Bishop a strong cast of eye which enables him, when he speaks, to address himself to nobody in particular; although, immediately after speaking, he turns on you a glance that conveys an expression of the most absolute impartiality.

It has been an old custom here for a number of students to reside with the Bishop. The practice is, I believe, a relic of that order of things in which almost all our pre-Reformation Universities arose; the habit, I mean, of having a school attached to the church (though *that* of course by itself is as old as the synagogue), and of having a separate body of clergy appointed to teach. There is, or was, such a foundation of teaching canons in connexion with the Parish Church of this place. The remains of a college still exist behind the Castle. Some Bishop, who was as much knight as minister, turned these into stables. As it is, Dr

Lightfoot has some six or seven young men in residence with him. They come here from Oxford and Cambridge for a year before ordination. Some have taken their degree in arts; others (according to the later custom, which allows one to occupy his undergraduate course entirely with divinity—an arrangement which saves theology at the sacrifice of general culture) others, I say, are bachelors in divinity. They have an ordered life in the Castle. Breakfast is at 7.45, and is followed by prayers in the Chapel at 8.15. Then one of the Chaplains lectures to the men from 9–10. For instance, this morning a Mr Southwell has been saying some things upon the genius of Hebrew poetry, previous to reading the first forty psalms, which is a subject of examination for Orders. Then follows an interval of two hours which is filled with reading, directed (by the Chaplain) to the foregoing lecture. Another lecture comes from 12–1. To-day my friend, Eden, will take introduction to the 1st Epistle of Peter, if his economic duties (for he is purser, caterer, steward, and I know not what all, to his chief) allow him any time. The Bishop is to lecture shortly on principles of textual criticism. We dine at one. The afternoon is taken up with district visiting. Each man has a little plot of ground to work in the agricultural and mining country round. One evening a week is, I think, given by each to a cottage reading. Other nights these men help my friend in evening classes and recreations at an institute for lads in the town.

This, you will think, is a long, but I assure you it is a needful, interlude between telling you how beautiful a thing the bishop's household life is, and saying in so many words wherein its beauty lies.

He calls these lads (and I can imagine worse things than to feel myself, for the nonce, one of them) his family, and they treat him as frank, ingenuous English gentlemen's sons would treat their father. He is accessible to their difficulties and their doubts, if they have any; but, a thing more remarkable, he is open to all their kittenhood of mirth and fun. To hear him alone with them is to feel you are on the edge of a circle, which tempts you almost to stand on tiptoe and look over and wish you were inside. It is a searching trial of true homeliness, to observe how it comports itself when there are strangers present. But I assert my coming in has not bated one jot of all this family joy. Last evening after prayers, they were poking fun at the Bishop. One man was asked how he was getting on with Hebrew. The fellow boldly turned the weapon round by enquiring whether his lordship was prepared to teach him. Dr Lightfoot was gently demurring, when somebody else burst in, as if with a child's impatience and fear of some older uncompleted promise: "No, not before we have had these lectures on botany". Then, assuming the air of some one to whom that study was even as his necessary food, he went on to report his observations, taken daily on his walks to and from the district, of two *interesting weeds*. It sounded like a clever parody upon Darwin and his climbing plants trained up the bed-post.

I have written all this in order to show—if it is within the power of words to show a thing which lies more in the feeling of the whole, than in any enumeration, however complete, of the details—how happy an example one has here of the spirit and the action of the English Church. Within, you have a home and a beehive both in one; without, everything is plain, and simple, and strenuous. The Bishop preaches such sermons as the one I sent you. His Chaplains teach, and visit, and preach. The students are an earnest and healthy set of men. Nothing is allowed in the Castle which speaks of pomp or pretension. You go down morning and evening to prayers in the Chapel; I suppose it is about the finest palace chapel in Britain. A simple service is held. The Bishop and a Chaplain read the lessons and lead the prayers. Another Chaplain has trained a choir of boys from the neighbouring town. Behind these choristers sit the students; the Bishop's servants (eight I counted) are in the back seats. One or two from the outside also seem to attend. The psalms and hymns are simply but sweetly sung. So anxious is Dr Lightfoot that nothing should lie unused, nothing rest in an empty name, that I believe he is fitting up the Chapel with seats, so as to have a service every Sabbath. Much of what I have seen here, the earnestness and the manliness of the men, the order of the household, the thoroughness of the instruction, the devoutness of prayers, the sweetness of the singing, the beauty, the learning, the goodness, the simplicity make me hang my head for shame both as a man and as a minister; for my whole heart consents to these things that they are right.

And yet something within me always rises and says: Thou hast a better portion in the North than all these things if thou only knewest it. Thy God, thy father's God, hath wrought nobler things in Scotland than any that are here....

These thoughts have come to me to-day, since hearing the Bishop's beautiful prayer added (by his own hand and heart, I believe) to the morning service. He asked the Lord of the Universal Church mercifully to direct those who were now charged with the choice of a chief minister for the county of Northumberland, that they might appoint one who could set forward God's work in the district and further the salvation of all men. That was for the new Bishop of Newcastle, a see to which Dr Lightfoot has parted with a considerable part of his living....

AUCKLAND CASTLE,
May 1st, 1882.

I think my last letter ended on Friday night after service in the little Chapel at half-past nine. True family worship it was.

At 12 this forenoon I came up to the students' room and took notes of an oral lecture of Eden's on 1st Peter. It was a discussion of the ἐν Βαβυλῶνι ch. v, based on the Bishop's notes. At 1 we dined, and at 1.30 ran for the train to Durham, whither Eden had invited me to go with him for the afternoon.

Thou knowest—dost thou not?—the steep, picturesque little town that lies on the wooded Wear, the old and thronging bridge, the climb to the Castle—as precipitous, we said, as the ascent to Killiecrankie— the cottage, the old gateway, the open square, a retreat (like the Wartburg) from the busy town, with Dean's, Canons', Archdeacons' houses about. First we went through the cloisters and Cathedral to the Castle where the college now is. We explored the rooms of the "Union", saw the dining-hall and the pictures, and the places of state just vacated by the judges on circuit. Eden shewed me with a kind of rapture the rooms where the Bishop's party first resided on coming to Durham. The tapestries and carvings were very fine.

But by far the finest remained. About three we went into the Cathe- dral. An enthusiastic but sensible verger,...shewed us over it; and we joined in his praises as he passed from point to point of the history and the building....

After the service (about 5) it rained heavily. We sought refuge in Canon Tristram's, whose house is, like himself, a treasury of birds and beasts....From thence a hand-gallop brought us through the drenching rain to the station....

.   .   .   .   .   .

Yesterday morning the Bishop and his men all went to early com- munion in a neighbouring church. I rested till 8, and then joined them at 8.30 in the Chapel. After breakfast I went with Dr Lightfoot and

Mr Eden to one of the town's churches, where we had a simple easy service, and an earnest popular sermon from the words, "Whence then cometh wisdom?" The preacher shewed us how even in Job's day the devout heart felt through and behind all the phenomena of nature, and the explanations of these offered by men, and reached to an Eternal Power before which it bowed, and to which it trusted for a life beyond. It was beautiful to see the chief minister worshipping among his people, and going in and out before them like a true ποιμὴν λαοῦ.

Both sermons were *extempore*. It was beautiful to see the supper table in the evening with Dr Lightfoot. All his ministers and curates and students gathered about it, after the day's work was done. The evening worship was full of solemnity. You felt the influence of good men being all about you. "Verily God is in this place."

Chapter V

PERSONAL RECOLLECTIONS

THE above vivid picture by the Rev. Robert Barbour depicts the life at Auckland Castle, as seen by a visitor, fifty years ago.

The following seven stories written for this book in recent months record lasting impressions on very different minds. The writers, of whom two are Bishops and one a Dean, were all Sons of the House.

§ 1

With all his simplicity and playful humour, there was an air of moral grandeur about Bishop Lightfoot such as I never have met with in the presence of any other man.

The massive rugged vastness of his Cathedral seemed well suited as a setting for his greatness, and the grave solemnity of his utterance in his sermons. Never shall I forget hearing him in Auckland Chapel at my ordination say: "Forget me, forget the service of to-morrow, forget the human questioner. Transport yourselves in thought from the initial to the final enquiry. The great day of inquisition, the supreme moment of revelation is come. The Chief Shepherd, the Universal Bishop of souls is the questioner. It is no longer a matter of the making of the promises, but of the fulfilment of the promises. The 'Wilt thou' of the ordination day is exchanged for 'Hast thou' of the Judgment Day—'Hast thou been diligent in prayer?' 'Hast thou framed and fashioned thy life?'"[1]

And yet in the same Chapel I realised the intense love and humility of the Bishop. I came back to stay a night with one of the Curates at the Castle Lodge, and naturally went to Mattins in the Chapel, sitting alone in one of the stalls. The service ended; the Bishop and his little choir went out, and I remained for a quiet time on my knees. At length, as I stole out, I found to my astonishment that the Bishop was waiting behind the screen. He would not intrude upon a junior Curate

[1] *Ordination Addresses*, pp. 72–3.

at his prayers, but he would keep the Diocese waiting till he had given me a cordial handshake and word of good cheer.

§ 2

We had no doubts that if Lightfoot wished a thing, you must do it. You didn't argue whether it was right or wrong, you just had to do it because you could not disappoint his love. He meant you to keep your own judgment, and his humility would have made him pay the highest respect to your objections, but somehow you couldn't help feeling that the highest call was the call to meet his love by your acquiescence.

The other thing that was most noticeable about him was his simplicity. Both in his humour, and appreciation of humour, and in the little things of daily life, his simplicity came out. I remember a delightful scene one night at Auckland. An old clergyman of some position in the county had come over to stay, with his daughter. He was a little absent minded, and when we came out of Chapel he wanted to go to bed; and without the least thinking what he was doing, he went and lit a bedroom candle and handed it to the Bishop, who meekly took it and went to bed! It was an intensely comic scene, because the old Rector's daughter was so very conscious of what her father had done. The Bishop's meek acceptance was not only so delicately courteous, but so irresistibly droll. His sense of humour was always so perfectly natural, the frank way in which he accepted a joke that amused him, and that amazing laugh with which he went off.

I remember now the scene when he saw the soap advertisement caricature of Gladstone as the baby in the bath reaching out for the cake of soap; I can see him sitting in the corner of the sofa and going off in that loud crow of enjoyment. It was absolutely childlike.

I am quite sure that the love of the Diocese for him was the answer to that love of his.

If ever a man reflected in his character the Divine Love, if ever a man was great through his simplicity and through the childlike quality of his character, that man was Lightfoot. And after all, as one's experience of life goes on, one sees more and more that those are the two greatest qualities that a man can shew.

§ 3

Reverence for our great father in God is so strong in all of us that we shrink from writing any reminiscences of him which are unworthy or inadequate.

The Bishop, as we all know, did not allow himself any prolonged inactivity; his rest was chiefly change of occupation—resumption of literary work, which had been laid aside when he became Bishop. But there were "leisure moments" at Auckland, during which he loved to chat with his sons, and enjoy our jokes. One afternoon, in a leisure moment, he strolled over to the stables with his favourite collie, "Dugald". But trouble awaited him; for collie and mastiff fell out and fought. The Bishop intervened, and seizing them, apparently by the jaws, pulled them apart. I saw him pass my windows with face as white as a sheet. He could not stand the sight of blood. He was a sorry sight, with apron all torn, and bleeding a good deal from a bitten hand. The incident serves to illustrate his personal courage.

I was struck also by his coolness in danger of another sort. When we were staying with him in Oban, we hired a small open boat, and sailed round the Island of Kerrera. All went well till we were entering the Straits, at the south of the Island, when a violent squall struck us. Had the sheet been fast we should have been swamped, but it was let go in time, and, tumbling about in the choppy sea, we got the sail down and reefed it. The picture of the Bishop, with the MS. of his Ignatius in his hand, quite calm and self-possessed, seemed to me characteristic.

As we rowed up the Fjords in Norway, he would be working at his Epistle of Clement, every now and then looking up to admire some waterfall, or other striking feature of the scenery, which he considered more continuously beautiful than Switzerland.

The latter country he knew well, and must have been a fairly good climber, for he had done his 12,000 feet. At Oban, in 1883, he enjoyed some good walks across the mountains, preferring always to find out the route from the ordnance map rather than ask the way; and keenly interested in all the little mountain flowers, which he loved.

It was amusing when some frivolous person tried to draw him into some such discussion as whether —— ought to shave off his moustache at his approaching ordination. He would quaintly put up his eye-glass and call attention to some very ordinary object in the landscape, and evade the unnecessary reply. Most memorable of all the holidays was that time at Braemar, when Archbishop Benson and Dr Westcott were staying in the same place, and these three great men, old school-fellows, used to meet at the little Church for daily Service and arrange expeditions together. Returning from one of these, we met a carriage. The Bishop was first to recognise in it Queen Victoria, and bade us step aside with bare heads. She evidently recognised him with pleasure. Had not those two noble souls many points of spiritual affinity?

§ 4

I was driving the Bishop in a stolkjar along a rough road near the Romsdal Horn when he wished to cross from one valley to another. After a few miles the road became so narrow with rocks on one side, and a sheer drop into the lake on the other, that I said to him, "I wish you would climb out at the back of the vehicle, there is only about 4 inches to spare on the near side". The Bishop looked down the preci-pice, and after a moment's pause remarked, " Other stolkjars must have taken this road. Drive on"—and continued to correct proofs which he had that morning received.

In spite of his sedentary life he was capable of great exertion at times, thinking nothing of ascending Lochnagar from Braemar when he must have been nearly 60 years old. I always felt, however, that it was the long tramp without a proper meal near the Romsdal Horn in Norway which was the beginning of the break-up of his health.

§ 5

The Bishop's fearlessness was again shewn when in 1885 he visited Sicily in order to explore certain churches, especially at Trapani. On his way out he made the ascent of Vesuvius with two of us. The mountain was uneasy, and throwing up hot ashes and lava about every three or four minutes. The guides on the upper cone refused to take visitors to the actual edge of the crater, except for an exorbitant fee.

The Bishop, however, would look into the crater. He began to walk steadily up by himself and we went with him. Seeing his determina-tion, a guide ultimately accompanied us, and choosing a calm interval allowed us to look over for a moment into the crater, himself holding on to the Bishop's coat-tails. Little but smoke and steam could be seen. But the Bishop lingered and had to be literally dragged away just as a peculiarly vicious puff scattered ashes and sticky red hot lava all around us. The Bishop was quite unmoved.

§ 6

To explain Lightfoot's attraction for me, and how I came to throw in my lot with the Auckland Brotherhood, I am afraid I must go back a little to Cambridge days, and even before. I had been used to a village Church and a school Chapel where the services were of the simplest sort, and I shrank from anything the least elaborate; and somewhere in this instinctive shrinking I put Theological Colleges, where I imagined everyone would be turned out after a pattern, and that one I should not like.

It was against this background that I heard of Lightfoot, who had no college such as I dreaded and simply gathered men round him—men of the sort I could take to—and sent them to work in his Diocese. So I wrote to a student at the Castle whom I knew slightly asking if I should have any chance of being accepted and what I ought to do. Then came an invitation, visit and interview, and from that day forward I had neither doubt nor fear—my life's course was settled.

Nothing particular happened, as far as I remember; there was nothing noteworthy about the interview—it was just sympathetic and kindly. But I was captured. The man and his surroundings, i.e. the men and their spirit, appealed to me tremendously. Specially I remember being thrilled by the Chapel and compline, and it was borne in upon me once and for all that here was something well worth belonging to for life and whatever lay beyond life....

Of course, Lightfoot himself was the central inspiration yet I do not think I ever felt quite at home with him, or entirely at ease in his company, though I was with him once in Norway and had good opportunities—perhaps because I was as shy as he was. But the point is that I never felt this mattered in the least. It was enough to know he cared and to try to please him. I mostly talked about the other Auckland men, and their doings of the lighter sort, and that always interested him. Once I remember, when I told him, how as a monitor at school, I had caned others, but rather regretted not having had the experience of being caned myself, he humorously suggested that it was not too late to make good that defect.

Truly he was a great chief, direct and simple and strong, and he made us feel that we would go anywhere and do anything (or anyhow attempt it) for his sake, for we knew it was for Christ's sake, Christ's Church in the Diocese of Durham which, as it was his, was our pride and joy.

§ 7

I went to Auckland Castle in 1887 and was there till the Christmas of that year. I was rather raw; plenty of good intentions; some brains, but raw distinctly.

Very well, what did Auckland do?

I should say that Auckland was different from anything else I ever came across. It was not School—there were no lessons—few lectures— no Masters or Headmasters. It was not like College—Tutors and Deans were unknown.

I think the most striking thing was that Auckland was Lightfoot, and Lightfoot was Auckland. For me he permeated and dominated the whole thing. It was not that he said much, or did much, but he was IT. With all the camaraderie of the Brotherhood, Auckland was never to me that same place, even under Westcott.

As is well known, Lightfoot had no beauty of face or form, but he had a most gorgeous smile, and when this came, it lit up his face like a glory and made it fine. I used to save up funny stories to tell just in order to conjure up that smile. It transformed the man.

The next thing I single out is that, with all the love he inspired, that love involved reverence. Not by thought, word, or deed would I ever lose respect for him. He would meet me on terms which I knew were as equal as man could get to man. There was no standing on the dignity of office, or learning, or personality. It is easy for youth in such cases to be over-familiar: I like to think that I never overstepped the mark. I remember that on one occasion a visitor spoke and acted in a way which we thought was too familiar. We were furious. Then essentially it was the personality and example of Lightfoot that affected me. We read, we worked, because Lightfoot was working and reading. We were no longer undergraduates, rather cocksure, and full of theories, and panaceas. We learnt humility of the right sort and never forgot it.

Just the right setting of the whole thing were the Compline services in Auckland Chapel. The silent Chapel with Lightfoot in his place —"The Lord Almighty grant us a quiet night and a perfect end, Amen"—"Brethren be sober, be vigilant; because your adversary, the devil, walketh about as a roaring lion seeking whom he may devour:

whom resist steadfast in the faith"—And the hymn "The day Thou gavest, Lord, is ended"....

> "So be it, Lord, Thy throne shall never
> Like earth's proud empires pass away.
> Thy kingdom stands, and grows for ever
> Till all Thy creatures own Thy sway."

And so we learnt faith and hope.

For ourselves; I do not know whether it was ever said to me in so many words, but it is as clear as if it had been spoken:

"The unwritten law of the Brotherhood is this; you go where you are sent, you work till you drop, the Bishop will shew you no sort of preference or notice, but...you have your place in the Bishop's prayers"

—and it was enough, I asked for no more, I expected less.

When the time came for ordination, I was asked where I would like to go, and the answer was pat of course, "The Bishop can send me wherever he likes, but if it is all the same to him, I would prefer a big town and poor people". I got drafted off to a slum in a town. I was only there eighteen months. Six months after my ordination to the priesthood, I was invited to take charge of the Mission in South London of my old College. I did my best to get out of it. I consulted Canon Body and others. I could not get anyone to say "Don't go". In desperation, I went to Lightfoot. He heard me patiently. He said very little, but he did say, "I think a College has a claim on its members". I met someone outside who said, "Well, what is the result?" My only answer was, "I'm going". And so my connexion with the Diocese of Durham came to an end.

Perhaps I ought to add that, just as I trusted the Bishop, I felt I was trusted. Others probably will put this side better.

I was ordained Priest by Kennion, then of Adelaide, in 1888 because Lightfoot was ill. That illness hit me like a knockdown blow.

If by the mercy of God I meet Lightfoot once more, I hope to goodness he will not say anything by way of praise. I don't think he is in the least likely to forget, but I'd like him to smile.

ST PETER'S CHAPEL, AUCKLAND CASTLE

(This Medieval Banqueting Hall was consecrated as a Chapel on St Peter's Day, 1665, by Bp. Cosin, and greatly adorned by Bishop Lightfoot)

Chapter VI

SAINT PETER'S DAY

NO record of Bishop Lightfoot would be complete without a description of his annual gathering of his "sons" at Auckland Castle on St Peter's Day.

What he thought of this Brotherhood is clearly expressed in his letter[1] to Archbishop Benson on January 31st, 1885, when his name had been mentioned as a possible successor to Bishop Jackson at London. He could not possibly have gone, he says,

The wrench of leaving Durham would be even worse than the wrench that brought me here, for an ideal is gradually forming itself of which I can only say that I wish I had the grace and power in any degree to realise it. But it has its centre in the work and men gathered about me at Auckland Castle; and this would hardly be possible elsewhere.

And he wrote to one of his "sons":

It is a real joy to me to hear you so appreciated St Peter's Day. To me it is the great day of the year, and I hope it will grow in value both to my sons and myself.

The day was always heralded by this letter from the Bishop some weeks before:

AUCKLAND CASTLE,
BISHOP AUCKLAND.

My dear...

As St Peter's Day is fast approaching, I write to remind you that I am looking forward to the pleasure of seeing you. I trust that you will consider this a paramount engagement to which all others will be postponed, so that we may meet in as large numbers as possible.

[1] *Life of Edw. White Benson, Abp.*, II, 46.

Try and be here if you can in time for the evening meal at half past seven o'clock on Tuesday the 28th.

Yours affectionately,

J. B. DUNELM.

With such a welcome in store, we started from our various lodgings—and meeting one and another *en route* we arrived at Auckland, and hastened, as sons of the house, through the side door and up to the great dining-room where the Bishop greeted us with an eager grasp of the hand. One year it happened that two of our brethren had grown their beards, and by good fortune they met, each rather embarrassed, in the Bishop's presence. To the delight of the bystanders he came to their rescue and introduced them to one another.

The usual programme was as follows:

On the Eve of St Peter's Day:

7.30 p.m.	Supper.
9.30	Evening Prayer.

On St Peter's Day:

8.0 a.m.	Holy Communion.
9.0	Breakfast.
11.0	Morning Prayer and Address by the Bishop.
1.15 p.m.	Lunch.
2.0	Photograph.
5.0	Tea on the Lawn.
8.0	Dinner.
9.30	Evening Prayer.

Next Morning:

7.20 a.m.	Breakfast for early train.
8.0	Morning Prayer.

A unique feature of the gathering was that large spaces

SAINT PETER'S DAY 51

were purposely arranged for informal intercourse, which
did so much to strengthen bonds of friendship.

The bare outline recalls precious memories of crowded
friendships. Wandering round the terraces in the long
summer night comparing notes with one, you suddenly
met another and another, whom you had not seen for a
year. And then stealing into the glorious Chapel you
found a place and the service began; a Chaplain reading
prayers, and the Bishop in his stall.[1]

When prayers were ended, a holy stillness crept over
us as we stayed, with the evening light just enough to
reveal the Saxon saints in the windows, and the row of
later Bishops' names and coats of arms painted along the
North and South Walls.

Coming out quietly one by one, we found the Bishop
chatting to a group in the drawing-room; then saying
"Good-night" he was off to his study. Later in the
Chaplain's room, or the servants' hall (now Library)
there gathered a merry symposium of brethren.

Next morning at 8 o'clock in the Chapel the Bishop
came attended by his Chaplains: Eden, Savage, Southwell, Armitage Robinson, Banton, Harmer, or Welch.

As year after year we knelt there, the mystery and the
glory seemed to increase, and new resolves put new
meaning into the usual offertory hymn:

Holy offerings...
On Thine altar laid we leave them,
Christ present them, God receive them.

[1] The Bishop's stall used to have a canopy and curtains of red material,
rather dingy, but at a meeting of the brethren in the drawing-room on St
Peter's Day 1886, it was agreed to subscribe for a new oak canopy to be
given to the Bishop. This is now a handsome addition to Cosin's Screen, and
bears the inscription:

EX: DONO: FILIORUM: DOMUS:
A: S: M.D.CCC.LXXX.VII:

4-2

Then breakfast, and after it many a talk, and not a little tobacco on the terrace, or the great lawn, or indoors till Morning Prayer.

Who that was present can ever forget the Bishop reading the Lesson?—the very sound of his voice comes back:

So when they had broken their fast, Jesus saith to Simon Peter, Simon son of John, lovest thou Me?...He saith unto him, Feed my lambs....Follow thou Me.

Then the Sermon, when the Bishop, often with voice breaking with emotion, seemed to take every individual in the whole Brotherhood to his heart as he spoke in such words as:

The touch of Christ, the voice of Christ, the look of Christ, but above all the prayer of Christ! "I have prayed for thee." What else shall we need if only we realise this! Christ interceding for me, Christ concentrating His prayer on me, Christ individualising His merits for me, Christ pleading for me His atoning blood before the Eternal Throne![1]

"Fight the good fight, with all thy might", one of our "Auckland Hymns", would follow. Its four strong verses form an expansion of the Bishop's chosen motto ἀνδρίζεσθε κραταιοῦσθε (1 Cor. xvi. 13) and to sing it in that Chapel filled with brothers after such a Sermon was an inspiration. Fellowship in Christ seemed vocal and intensely real. That hymn became a sort of "slogan" of the Brotherhood, and to sing it in a Bible Class of men was to pass on the secret of the Chapel to the parish.

The photograph which came after lunch was certainly one of the events of the year, and grew more and more to be an outward sign of deepening fellowship.

The Annual Cricket Match became a fixture of increasing importance. In early days it was "Oxford versus

---

[1] *Ordination Addresses*, p. 135.

Cambridge", then later a more important distinction developed and the match was between "Married and Single". And later still, long after Bishop Lightfoot's day, there came a match of "Bishops against Clergy". As there were but nine Bishops, two (one of them a Metro‑politan) were allowed a second innings—and the result of the match established the fact that the Priests were "inferior clergy".

At tea on the lawn, various parish friends came to meet old students who had worked in their districts.

At length we assembled for Evensong in the Chapel, and more than once the service was used for the admis‑sion of one or other of the "sons" to a new charge. Before the Bishop's final blessing, we would sing "The day Thou gavest, Lord, is ended", a hymn whose melody is enriched with St Peter's Day associations.

Such was the glorious day. The grand state bedrooms took on something of the air of school dormitories, and the lawns the look of college playing fields; and the great historic dining‑room had never seen more festive gather‑ings than when Dr Lightfoot sat down with his "sons" at meals. The day was one long re‑union of his family for worship, fellowship and play.

And yet, though he thus made us feel that it was for him "the greatest day of the year", it was actually while we were all about him that he finished the great book for which the learned world had for years been waiting, *Nulla dies sine linea!*

The Preface to the three volumes of the *Apostolic Fathers* is dated "S. Peter's Day, 1885". To read that Preface, and picture him completing it amid the scenes we have been describing is most suggestive.

After a rapid review of his thirty and more years' work,

in the course of which he has arrived conclusively at the opinion of the genuineness of the Seven Epistles of Ignatius, he proceeds to "express my obligations to many personal friends and others who have assisted me in this work":

My thanks are especially due to Dr W. Wright, who has edited the Syriac and Arabic texts, and whose knowledge has been placed freely at my disposal, wherever I had occasion to consult him; to Professor Guidi who, though an entire stranger to me, transcribed for me large portions of Coptic texts from manuscripts in the Vatican; to Mr P. le Page Renouf, the well-known Egyptian scholar, who has edited the Coptic Version of the Ignatian Acts of Martyrdom from Professor Guidi's transcript; and to Bryennios the Metropolitan of Nicomedia, whose name has recently gathered fresh lustre through the publication of the *Didache*, and to whom I owe a collation of the Pseudo-Ignatian Epistles from the same manuscript which contains that work. I am also indebted for important services...to Dr Bollig the Sublibrarian of the Vatican, to Dr Zotenberg the keeper of the Oriental Manuscripts in the Paris Library, to Professor Wordsworth of Oxford, and to Dr Oscar von Gebhardt the co-editor of the *Patres Apostolici*.

Here is by far the most learned Bishop of his day, the acknowledged leader among his peers, the great scholars of Europe, in the act of at last being able to hand to the world the monumental results of his lifelong labours— and yet! with leisure that very day to devote his whole heart and mind to his sons in their home which he gave them at Auckland.

And the Auckland Family shall have their representa-tive among his learned helpers: "Lastly I have been relieved of the task of compiling the indices by my Chaplain the Rev. J. R. Harmer, Fellow of King's College, Cambridge, to whom my best thanks are due".

IN THE DIOCESE

"One of the greatest prelates who ever held the See of Durham.

...he did not believe that any diocese could be pointed out in which there was so much hearty concurrence of mind and action for religious objects as there was amongst all his clergy and laity under the guidance of the late Bishop."

DEAN LAKE OF DURHAM

proposing the restoration of the Chapter House in memory of Bishop Lightfoot. Feb. 18th, 1890.

Chapter VII

THE BISHOP IN THE DIOCESE

THE SCHOLAR AS BISHOP

WHEN the new Bishop and his Chaplains first came to Durham, they were met by Dean Lake at the North Road Station. Their heavily laden landau was taken carefully down the winding hill from the station, and over Framwellgate Bridge. Then suddenly, as if by a pre-arranged understanding, the horses broke into a hand-gallop up the narrow streets to the South Bailey. Thence through the narrow badly paved Dun Cow Lane they came at full gallop across Palace Green to Bishop Cosin's porch of the great hall of the Castle.

When the Bishop remarked on the risk of such driving, the Dean reassured him by saying that his coachman was an old Crimean gunner.

As they alighted, they found all the leading men of Durham University awaiting their new Visitor in caps and gowns, as though to assure him that there were students at Durham as eager to listen to him as at Cambridge.

But as the Bishop pointed out in a happy speech at the luncheon after his enthronement, there could not be the same opportunities in his case for learning now. This difference he illustrated by the contrast between the coats of arms of Cambridge and Durham. In both shields there were four lions, but while those at Cambridge were passant, those at Durham were rampant. And there is a book in the centre of the Cambridge shield "but when I look at the Durham arms, the book is gone".

Yet Durham was to see the publication of three volumes of the Bishop's greatest book, on the *Apostolic Fathers*. Though not published while he was at Cambridge, the greater part of it had all been in type for ten years, under constant revision, before it appeared in 1885.

Soon after it came out Bishop Fraser of Manchester got hold of it. He was dangerously ill, and only allowed to sit and read. While reading the Epistle of St Ignatius to the Ephesians, the Rector of his parish came in, "Listen to this, Rector", said the Bishop, and read aloud,

εἷς ἰατρός ἐστιν, σαρκικὸς καὶ πνευματικός, γεννητὸς καὶ ἀγέννητος, ἐν ἀνθρώπῳ Θεός, ἐν θανάτῳ ζωὴ ἀληθινή, καὶ ἐκ Μαρίας καὶ ἐκ Θεοῦ, πρῶτον παθητὸς καὶ τότε ἀπαθής, Ἰησοῦς Χριστὸς ὁ Κύριος ἡμῶν[1].

"Isn't it wonderful", he went on, "to think of Ignatius centuries ago cheering his friends at Ephesus with the same triumphant trust in Christ overcoming death that you and I have ourselves to-day."

Next morning, October 18th, 1885, as he was dressing, Bishop Fraser suddenly died—so one of the first uses of Lightfoot's *Apostolic Fathers* was to encourage a brother Bishop as he entered the Valley of the Shadow of Death. When he was told the story, Bishop Lightfoot listened with great interest and suddenly turned aside to hide his emotion.

The Judge's Rooms in Durham Castle had been placed at his disposal, and here he and his Chaplains

---

[1] "There is one only physician, of flesh and of spirit, generate and ingenerate, God in man, true Life in death, Son of Mary and Son of God, first passible and then impassible, Jesus Christ our Lord." *Epistle of Ignatius to the Ephesians*, 7 (Lightfoot's translation, II, i, 541).

resided while Auckland Castle was being prepared for them. Those eight springtide weeks at Durham are full of pleasant memories. They brought the Bishop into happy relations with the University, and he would frequently dine in Hall.

A glance at the Agenda of the Diocesan Conference of 1880 is a revelation of the wide and solid foundations of Church work and life that Bishop Lightfoot laid in the first year of his episcopate. That Diocesan Conference was itself the first gathering of the kind ever called together in the Diocese of Durham. The membership was based, as will be seen, on Ruridecanal representation, with a view to which the Deaneries were remodelled and Ruridecanal Conferences (as well as Chapters) were constituted.

All this, as well as the re-arrangements noted elsewhere of Ordinations and Confirmations and Church building, was started in the Bishop's first year, during which he was strenuously visiting his great Diocese of more than 100 miles from north to south.

He at once began preaching in the big towns and received a cordial welcome everywhere. There was a touch of distinction about him, which, coupled with the unique tradition of the Northumbrian Church, in which he delighted, seemed to give a special significance to the characteristic northern welcome he received. His absolute simplicity of manner, without detracting from a natural dignity of voice and appearance, went straight home to all those warm-hearted folk. Even the humblest lost all constraint in approaching him. At Monkwearmouth Church, for example, there was a typical verger. On the Bishop's first visit a small new house was pointed out, which the neighbouring squire, well known as always having his own way, had built overlooking the Church. Turning to the verger, the Bishop said, "I wonder *you* allowed Sir Hedworth Williamson to build that house so near". The man instantly replied, "Sir 'Edworth would ha' built 'is 'ouse on your 'ead, my Lord, if 'e'd 'ad a mind".

THE SEE OF NEWCASTLE

The first great undertaking to which the Bishop turned his attention was the division of the Diocese. This was no sudden proposal. Bishop Baring had submitted the question to all his Ruridecanal Chapters in 1876. Their judgment was almost unanimous as to the advisability of creating a new See. Then in 1877 the late Mr Thomas Hedley bequeathed the residue of his estate, amounting to some £17,000, as the nucleus of the necessary fund.

On March 26th, 1878, the Bishoprics Bill for Liver- pool, Newcastle, Southwell and Wakefield came up for the second reading. Bishop Baring supported it, effec- tively answering Lord Houghton's arguments against it not without humour and skill. It seems clear as one reads his speech that the Bishop had only been converted by the facts of the case, and perhaps against his inclination. He pointed out that the county of Durham had experienced a very rapid increase in population in recent years, and now counted about 1,000,000 inhabitants.[1] The number of benefices had doubled in the previous fifty years. He supported the Bill though he personally felt keenly the separation from Northumberland, where he had received much kindness. "But", he added, "there was a strong feeling in the country that the separation was of such

[1] "Comprises a million and a quarter," Bishop Lightfoot's opening speech, Diocesan Conference, 1880.

importance, and of such lasting benefit to the Church of England, that he had unwillingly consented to it."[1]

So the Act was passed, and the new Bishop from the first frankly adopted the proposal as already decided: "When I accepted the See of Durham", he told his first Diocesan Conference in September 1880, "it was re-presented to me that the formation of the new See was imminent, and this expectation weighed greatly with me". Even before he left Cambridge he secured, in a personal interview, the generous support of the Duke of Northumberland for the scheme. And in the summer of 1880 he brought from the South one of his examining Chaplains, the Rev. H. W. Watkins, then Warden of St Augustine's College, Canterbury, to be Archdeacon of Northumberland, and as such to take a prominent part in the organisation of the appeal to the Diocese, and "in nine months the work was practically done".

At the Church Congress in Newcastle in 1881, Bishop Fraser of Manchester expressed the general feeling when he said in his Sermon in the future Cathedral, "We wait eagerly to hear what our President has to say to-day".

In his Inaugural Address the President entered into no details, but showed that the scheme was practically launched:—

"Newcastle is destined before long to assume greater prominence in the eyes of Churchmen as the See of a new Diocese. At such a moment the session of the Congress at Newcastle is specially well timed. The reception of a large Representative Assembly of the Church will fitly close the history of the ancient Diocese of Durham. The old See will be fortified by the presence of the Congress for the severance and the new See will be ushered in amid the happiest auguries.[2]"

[1] Hansard, March 26th, 1878, Bishoprics Bill, House of Lords, Second Reading.
[2] *Church Congress Report*, 1881.

A week later came a letter, solving the problem of where the new Bishop was to live, from Mr J. W. Pease, a Newcastle banker, and a prominent member of the Society of Friends. This letter reveals the enthusiasm of the community for the scheme, and the way in which Bishop Lightfoot had captured all hearts:

Dear Mr Archdeacon,

So many people tell me that Benwell Tower is the most suitable place for the new Bishop that I think you ought to have it. Funds do not come in very quickly, and the purchase of such a house as you require must, therefore, be a difficulty. This being the case, I have concluded to hand the place over to the Committee, and as it is not occupied, they are very welcome to the possession at once, so that any alterations which may be considered needful, may be made without loss of time, and their solicitor can communicate with mine as to the conveyance.

Churchmen and Quakers used not to get on very well together, but those times are past, and I most sincerely trust that the important step about to be taken may be in every way successful. What I propose to instruct my solicitor to convey is the Tower, with its garden, old burial ground, stables and lodge; and as many of the cottages near the stables as you may require. . . .

Yours very truly

JOHN PEASE

Then there came another £10,000 from Mr Spencer of Ryton, and a committee of ladies got together a gift of furniture for Benwell Tower.

So, on St James' Day 1882, three years and a quarter after his own consecration, the Bishop had the satisfaction of taking part in the consecration, in Durham Cathedral, of Dr Ernest Roland Wilberforce as the first Bishop of Newcastle.

REORGANISING "THE BISHOPRICK"

Meanwhile organisations had been rapidly developing in the county of Durham. The old "Officialty" of the Dean and Chapter, which had exercised archidiaconal jurisdiction over thirty-six parishes in Durham, was abolished, and the new Archdeaconry of Auckland formed.

The seven unwieldy Rural Deaneries revived by Bishop Longley, twenty-five years before, were remodelled into twelve more workable centres (there are now four-teen) to meet the altered conditions of larger populations, and the access of laymen to the Conferences.

The authoritative document then drawn up by Bishop Lightfoot, and issued to each Rural Dean on appoint-ment, setting forth their duties, has been adopted by each of his successors and is in use to-day.

There was no part of his work that weighed more on his heart, or had more lively interest for him, than his Confirmations: "I can honestly say that of all my epis-copal duties this is the one which gives me the most happiness". He augmented the number of centres, so that instead of biennial, or even triennial Confirmations, often at inconvenient centres, every parish had the chance of a Confirmation each year within reasonable distance. His plan which is still working was simplicity itself. He always gave two addresses to the candidates, dwelling on the twofold aspect of the Rite.

What a labour it was to him is revealed by the astonish-ing figures. In his ten years, there were 456 Confirma-tions. Frequently he held two services a day, and often with 250 or 300 candidates at each service. But for the aid of Bishop Parry of Dover in his first year, he faced all this work single-handed till his last year, when Bishop Sandford of Tasmania came to his aid, as Rector of Boldon and assistant Bishop. But still he went on. There came a great Confirmation Service at Sunderland Parish Church when the Bishop almost broke down. He had to rest again and again during the laying-on of hands.

A LAY MINISTRY

One of the most remarkable features of the Bishop's work in the Diocese was his activity among the Laity. First he set himself to bring them into closer touch with the Church by giving them a new and effective voice in her Councils; and secondly he called into being a trained body, not only of Lay Readers in the ordinary parochial sense, but of Lay Preachers with a wider Commission for the Rural Deanery and Diocese.

1. It must be remembered that in those days the Laity had but small voice in the Church's consultations. There were few, if any, Ruridecanal Conferences, apart from Chapters for Clergy only. Convocation, for the most part, attracted little interest. Church Congresses were entirely unofficial. It was then that Bishop Lightfoot, at his very first Diocesan Conference in 1880, struck a note which foreshadows the immense developments familiar to us now in the Lay House of the Church Assembly. "There are forces operating which render it more than ever advisable that the Church of England should habituate herself to corporate action."[1] This ideal he never ceased to proclaim. Five years later in his charge to the Clergy, he again said, "There are many among us— I confess that I am one—who yearn for the time when the

[1] *Durham Diocesan Calendar* 1881, pp. 93, etc.

Church of England, as a whole, shall have a general representative Assembly ".

He had already set on foot, as a first step, the election of laymen to serve on the Ruridecanal and Diocesan Con^ference. Alluding to this he says:

The interest created by this exceeded my best hopes. There was much discussion whether the electors should be Communicants, or at least members of the Church of England, or parishioners assembled in Vestry. The latter course was adopted, and worked well.

All this produced a sympathetic interest in the revival of corporate life. It is specially interesting to witness the active interest of the Laity. Without their counsel and support the work of the Clergy would be maimed and crippled indeed. I will say no more than this—They— the Laity—must feel that they no less than the Clergy are bound, each in his vocation and ministry, to promote the knowledge of God's truth, and the extension of Christ's Kingdom; and it would be little short of an insult to suggest by words of special commendation that they were doing some great thing, when they thus claim their share in the respon^sibilities of active Churchmanship.[1]

These ideals for corporate action on the part of the Church were not reached for nearly forty years. But the Bishop is here clearly seen as one of the pioneers of the Church Assembly.

2. Almost simultaneously with this invitation of the Laity to new consultative functions, as soon as ever the new See of Newcastle was formed he called them to more directly spiritual ministrations both as Lay Readers, and especially in a new way as Lay Evangelists. His vision of what laymen might do, as sharers in the priest^hood of all believers, may be seen from his repeated utterances on the subject. We select the following.

At his first Diocesan Conference in 1880 he says:

... This leads me to speak of a subject which I regard as supremely important at this crisis in the history of our Church. I mean the

[1] *Dioc. Calendar*, 1881, p. 95.

organisation of lay agency. The subject will come up for discussion this afternoon, and I trust it will be thoroughly sifted.

. . . .

Even if the supply of Clergy were largely increased it would still be unable to meet the growing demand for spiritual ministrations. Look at the extensive rural parishes of Northumberland...the thronged parochial districts of Newcastle with perhaps 15,000 inhabitants. How is it possible for an Incumbent, with even two or three curates (an almost ideal staff of clergy) to pierce effectively those densely welded masses of human beings? And so again with our colliery parishes, which stand midway between these extremes, where there is perhaps a central village or town, as a nucleus, with several outlying colonies of pitmen. Nothing but lay agency—and this on a very large scale—will meet these varied needs. What organisation is necessary for this purpose? What orders or offices should be created or revived? What functions should be assigned to them? What recognition should they receive? What qualifications should be imposed? What form of admission should be instituted? These are the questions open for discussion.

Having thus opened the subject he gave the Conference a free hand in debate, placing it second only in importance to the division of the Diocese. This recognition of a Lay Ministry of preaching was a new and somewhat startling departure. It was by no means universally welcomed. "There is need", he said, "of frankness, for it is only by the frank interchange of opinions that any real progress can be made. But there is need also of moderation, of forbearance, of sympathy, of the stedfast resolve to understand the position, and respect the motives of those who differ from ourselves." But in spite of some adverse feeling, he never wavered from his first conception of the value of this direct ministry of Lay Preaching. Again and again he returns to the subject in words of the deepest conviction.

Speaking at the inaugural meeting of a Junior Clergy Society in the Diocese in 1884 he says:

There is another problem of the day, which I earnestly commend to your serious attention. I refer to the employment and organisation of lay work in the service of Christ. I feel absolutely certain that in this lies the great hope of the future. We shall only thus secure that strength and diffusion of ministerial agency which will enable us to reach the masses: and what is hardly less important, we shall only thus bind to the Church that large body of men, who at present hang loosely to it, and will certainly drift elsewhere if the Church fails to find employment for their spiritual energies. Incorporate them into the *life* of the Church by entrusting to them the *work* of the Church. Then, and then only, will they feel what they owe to the Church.

Keep this problem ever before you. It must have a solution somehow. And if the larger aspects of the question require wide experience and patient waiting, can you not meanwhile do something, each of you, in your own little sphere? Might not more rapid progress be secured, if the clergy made a point of fastening upon the more promising boys, and young men of their flock, of concentrating a larger amount of attention on these, of gradually introducing them to work, and thus educating them as fresh centres of evangelisation? If this were done systematically, a geometric progression would be substituted for an arithmetic in the spiritual growth of the parish.

Once more, alluding to a large gathering of Lay Readers and Evangelists at Sunderland in his Charge[1] in 1886 he thus pressed the matter once more upon the Clergy:

I was deeply impressed by the earnestness and sobriety of tone which marked the speakers, and I felt that I should incur a grave responsibility if I did not do all in my power to encourage a movement which seemed to be the prompting of the Holy Spirit, and which held out hope of so much spiritual usefulness. . . .But your evangelist, it may be said, bears a strong likeness to the Wesleyan local preacher. I am not ashamed of the resemblance, I freely confess my admiration of the marvellous capacity of organisation which distinguished John Wesley, and which he has bequeathed to his followers. The truest Churchmen are those whose minds are most open to the lessons which can be gathered from all quarters. I believe that the Church of England has a greater power

[1] Charge delivered to the Clergy of the Diocese of Durham, November 25th, 1886.

of utilising the evangelistic zeal of her lay members, than any other Christian community, though hitherto it has been latent. Certainly this ought to be the case, for the sense of corporate unity with her, if she is true to her principles, is built upon a stronger and deeper foundation than accidental association for religious purposes. Most assuredly she will be wise to find employment for this zeal, for an untold mine of missionary power is here, which alone can cope with the spiritual destitution; and if neglected by her, this noble passion for Christ will seek relief for its yearnings in other channels. Most earnestly, therefore, do I recommend this movement.[1]

Meanwhile another new departure was set on foot. At a meeting of his Archdeacons and Rural Deans within eighteen months of his coming to Durham the Bishop appointed a committee to collect information on the

[1] The same spirit breathes in the short letter below, which was first issued in 1883 to each Lay Agent, and still is printed on their cards of membership:

"Dear Brothers and Sisters in Christ,

It has pleased God to put into your hearts the desire to dedicate your spare time to the service of the Sanctuary, and to the well-being of the flock of Christ.

Before all things give Him hearty thanks that He is thus leading you to realise your privileges as a royal priesthood, as living members of Christ's body.

Then ask yourselves how the seed thus sown in your hearts shall best bear fruit to the glory of His great Name.

In the first place, then, be loyal to your Church, and to your Clergy. 'Know them that labour among you, and are over you in the Lord.'

Next—strive to work harmoniously one with another, 'Be at peace among yourselves'.

Thirdly—there must be a consecration of the heart and mind, a consecration of the life to God. Christ, speaking of His disciples and friends, said, 'For their sakes I sanctify myself'. He is your pattern, sanctify yourselves also.

Lastly—there can be no true consecration of self where there is not prayer— prayer for the teaching of the Holy Spirit. 'Be ye therefore sober and watch unto prayer.'

These are the four pillars of a sound and effective ministration—loyalty, harmony, self-dedication, prayer.

May God give you grace to observe these things.

J. B. DUNELM."

Auckland Castle, 1883.

subject of Sisterhoods and Deaconesses. His next step was to appoint the Rev. George Body as Canon Missioner, and under him the work developed into what is now known as "The Society of Christ and the Blessed Mary the Virgin", an Association of Women for Church Work in the Diocese of Durham and elsewhere, with the sanction of the Bishop.

The Lay movement grew and gathered force as the years went on. Canon A. H. Patterson, who has served in the Diocese since the days of Bishop Baring, and who has for many years been the active secretary of the Lay Helpers' Association, has furnished details of its advance to the present day. Many commissions were issued for both Readers and Evangelists. Annual Services and Conferences for these were held, and were attended also by the Clergy and other Church workers. Careful examinations were instituted and Training Lectures given under a council of supervision in each Deanery. And every year, as a rule either at Durham or Auckland Castle, the Readers and Evangelists came into personal contact with their Bishop at a Conference upon their work, and enjoyed his hospitality and encouragement.

So securely and wisely were the foundations laid that the constitution Bishop Lightfoot created for the Durham Diocesan Lay Helpers' Association has persisted during the more than forty years since his death, with only such necessary modifications as were required by the growth of the work, especially by the need of Lay Ministrations in consecrated buildings owing to the present shortage of Clergy.

3. No apology is needed for adding to this account the following story from one of the Bishop's own choir boys. It illustrates his own characteristic method,

recommended to the junior Clergy of "fastening upon the most promising boys and young men" for ministerial training. It illustrates his love of youth, and his confidence in them. It illustrates (though this is not mentioned) his generosity towards many who would not otherwise have achieved their University education. And it gives one more fresh, almost boyish, picture of a side of the life at Auckland Castle under his genial rule.

It must be prefaced by a few words of explanation. As soon as he was settled in the Castle, the Bishop asked his Chaplain to find some boys for his choir. Mr Savage visited the Barrington School, where Mr Hammond, the Head Master, took him to the upper standard and explained to the boys that if they went to the Castle choir, it meant attending regularly every day, before breakfast. They would get coffee after service at the Castle, and then come to school. He then asked for volunteers. Two boys held up their hands—one of them is now a colonial Bishop and the other, a clergyman, is the author of the following account:

The Bishop always took a surprising interest in us, and through one of the Chaplains he expressed his wish to educate us. This offer was in some cases of course warmly accepted.

From time to time he would stroll in to the choir practices—much to our surprise.

On several occasions he took us into his study. I remember with what delight he produced Antony Beck's sword and with arm outstretched paced his room and said, "Can you imagine me marching at the head of my troops?" It was then that I received my first Church history lessons on St Aidan, "The Apostle of England", he called him. How thrilled I was with his stories of St Cuthbert.

One morning he was alone for Matins at 8.15—the Chaplains being away—and before the Vestry prayer he confessed to us that he was quite unable to lead the singing or accompany but he was sure we would do our best. Bob Hay—now Bishop of Tasmania—volunteered to lead, etc., and we all rose to the occasion. Psalms, Hymns and Responses were very well rendered. It was altogether most impressive. How we ran off to school afterwards with his praises ringing in our ears!

The memories of those services will never be effaced. The "musical" students provided the harmony and one read the First Lesson from one of the lofty Reading Pews, or Pulpits—"horse-boxes" we called them. The Bishop usually read the Second Lesson. We were spellbound as he translated direct from his Greek Testament. But then said someone, "Can you wonder? He is the greatest scholar in Europe. Look at his head!"

After Matins we got coffee in the kitchen and we supposed that it was on account of our boisterousness that the cook's face betokened her wrath. At any rate the quality of the coffee deteriorated and this was our opportunity. We decided to complain and jointly composed a letter to the Chaplain. This has been preserved I believe, for it caused immense amusement to His Lordship. An enquiry was instituted about the "dandelion" coffee we were sure was being served to us! At any rate we thought we had reformed matters.

We were always overjoyed when we knew there was to be an Institution Service and the solemnity thereof always impressed us and we soon learnt what it all meant.

The visit of all the Bishops from the Lambeth Conference was an event of amazing importance and we took part in the Service and intercessions for the division of the Diocese and the creation of the See of Newcastle.

The Park was our happy hunting ground, but on one occasion the Bishop called us all to him and in moving words expressed his grief that the eggs from a blackbird's nest round the lawn had been taken. Our guilt was undoubted, but we learnt our lesson and felt thoroughly ashamed of our conduct.

In the evening and on half holidays we spent our time on the cricket ground in the Park, and games were organised for us. The great match of the season was always against the Cathedral choir of Durham, and the Bishop frequently came to watch these struggles.

A terrific gale brought down many of the trees by the Park wall adjoining the ground. In one particular case the roots brought up a huge wall of earth with them and in vision we at once conceived the idea of a hut. Here at last was a good start—the hole dug out and the first wall *in situ*! Operations were at once commenced and our full strength was commandeered for them.

The structure was in our eyes to be exceeding magnifical and no detail was to be overlooked. Pit props carried the roofs made of turf sods, etc., "Of course we must have a fire place", and someone added: "There's a seam of coal on the cliffs by the river". This was duly "worked" and an old rusty fireplace put in position and all our labours were ended. Here was our Club House, which would also be our study where our "home lessons" would be tackled. The furniture was of the most primitive description and the accommodation—particularly when the fire smoked—can be readily imagined. At the best it was a dug-out of the roughest kind.

Our first caller was the Bishop, and we trembled when he expressed his wish to come in. He did so yet not without considerable difficulty and personal discomfort, for we laughed at his effort to crawl through the doorway. A vexatious down-draught did its worst and the atmosphere was appalling.

With the hut rules he was intensely amused, especially with the last one which stated that "*the subscription was* 1*d. per week but any member who gave more would be more thought of!*" There were others equally boy-like. They were preserved in the archives at the Castle for many years.

His Lordship then asked us—Hay, Bousfield and myself—about our work at school and at great length made us realise—for the first time—what was the purpose of our lessons, to form our characters and fit ourselves for the great game of life. How he opened our eyes as we hung on his words! It was a desire to serve that he put into our minds and from that moment the "call" came. We all won £60 Theological Scholarships at Durham University in successive years. Hay and I were ordained Priests at the Trinity Ordination 1894 at Auckland and shared the same room at the end of "Scotland"[1] in which Mr Eden had many years before given us our first Greek Testament Lesson (St John). Bousfield was not ordained but subsequently became Head Master of our old school—King James I Grammar School, Bishop Auckland.

THE LAMBETH CONFERENCE AND AUCKLAND

He was proud of the historic seat of the Bishops of Durham at Auckland Castle. In his Charge (November 1886) he thus refers to it:

[1] A wing in the Castle.

A large house enables Bishops to do many things conducive to efficient administration of the Diocese. I speak from experience. More over in some cases their residences have a high historical value. The Bishop's Manor House at Auckland is a notable example of this. It is, I believe, the oldest of episcopal residences. It has been connected with the Bishops of Durham from the time of the Conquest. It is associated with all the noblest memories of the See before and since the Reforma tion. It is still fresh with the impress of Cosin and Butler. Its Chapel is the most stately of episcopal Chapels, and it has been the joy and pride of the present occupant of the See to render the internal decorations worthy of the noble structure which he has inherited.

When he first took up his residence he had bought back several heirlooms which had been unwittingly included in the sale of his predecessor's effects; and after adding considerably to the gallery of portraits in the large drawing-room, he made, for preservation, a careful schedule of the property of the See as distinct from private ownership. Later on he wrote an illuminating pamphlet on the history of the place,[1] which established beyond a doubt, that, after the Restoration, Bishop Cosin had converted the great baronial hall into the existing Chapel, and to prove his contention Dr Lightfoot laid bare temporarily the foundations of the wing destroyed by Sir Arthur Hazlerigg which had contained the earlier double chapel.

But the crowning tribute to the love he felt for his official home was the embellishment of the interior of the Chapel itself. Here he had the advice of the Cathedral architect, Mr Hodgson Fowler of Durham, upon whose judgment he relied. One striking feature in this restora tion was the series of historical subjects which Messrs Burlison and Grylls introduced into the windows, representing scenes illustrating the evangelisation of the

[1] *Historical Essays*, Macmillan, 1895.

North of England from the time of St Oswald and St Aidan onwards. The Bishop took a special interest in selecting the subjects and supervising the details. To some of the historic figures were given the faces of personal friends in the Church of his own day.

The Lambeth Conference of 1888 was sitting when the work was completed, and he invited to the reopening of the Chapel a distinguished company of Archbishops, Metropolitans, and other Bishops from all parts of the Anglican Communion overseas to visit his Diocese and to rejoice with him. The occasion of this great assemblage is commemorated by a portrait-window placed later in the ante-chapel.[1] It is also recorded in the handsomely bound prayer-books, the gifts of the Bishop's guests, which adorn the stalls, with a Latin inscription[2] composed by his friend Dean Vaughan.

In connexion with this visit of the Bishops to Auck-land Castle in 1888, it is of special interest to notice the part taken by Bishop Lightfoot in the Lambeth Con-ference of that year.

The present Bishop of Durham writes: "I had occasion to refer to Stubbs' *Charges* this morning, and happened to come upon this reference to Bishop Light-foot's *rôle* in the Lambeth Conference, and it occurred to me that if you had not seen it, you might be glad to see how one great man impressed another":

Of those Bishops some few, even of the greatest, have been taken from us during the short time that has intervened: in particular the BISHOP

---

[1] See p. 93.
[2] Viro admodum Reverendo Josepho B. Lightfoot Episcopo Dunel-mensi Hoc quantulumcunque sit Studii Amicitiae Amoris Monumentum DD. DD. Fratres ab Omni Fere Orbis Terrarum Regione in Sacello Hospitali Nuper Refecto Congregati. Kal. sext. MDCCCLXXXVIII.
EN ΣΩMA KAI EN ΠΝΕΥΜΑ.

OF DURHAM, who in the leading part which he took in our delibera׳
tions, and by the authoritative wisdom, unwearied attention, and
elaborate work which were apparent in every word he said and every
line he indited in connection with the Conference showed himself a
very chief in counsel, pre׳eminent in ability and service, as in learning
and devotion.[1]

Bishop Stubbs of Chester had special opportunities of
observing what he has described, for he was Chairman
of the Committee on Divorce, of which Bishop Light׳
foot was a member.

Our Bishop also was Chairman of the Committee on
Purity. Their Report was entirely his work and was said
to have been unique in having been unanimously
adopted without alteration "as expressing the mind of
the Conference on this great subject".

It is an example of the "authoritative wisdom, un׳
wearied attention, and elaborate work" of which Bishop
Stubbs speaks.

The Report differs from all the others in its style, for,
where the others are all for the most part in oblique
narration, the whole of this one is couched in direct
speech, that it might "go forth as the utterance of the
United Conference".

Archbishop Davidson, when he welcomed the Auck׳
land Brotherhood to Lambeth in 1923, told us he never
could forget our Bishop's speech introducing that Report
at this Lambeth Conference.

The Archbishop also told us that for weeks beforehand
our Bishop had taken a large share in the preparatory
work. And the wording of the Encyclical Letter was
mainly the work of Lightfoot, Stubbs and himself, when
he was Dean of Windsor, and Secretary of the Con׳

---

[1] Bishop Stubbs, *Visitation Charges*, p. 124.

ference. They sat up the best part of two whole nights in the Lollard's Tower doing it.

Bishop Lightfoot acknowledged that all this had completely overtaxed his strength:

> While I was suffering from overwork and before I understood the true nature of my complaint, it was the strain both in London and at home in connection with this Pan-Anglican gathering that broke me down hopelessly. I did not regret it then. I do not regret it now. I should not have wished to recall the past even if my illness had been fatal. For what after all is the individual life in the history of the Church? Men may come and men may go—individual lives float down like straws on the surface of the waters till they are lost in the ocean of eternity, but the broad, mighty rolling stream of the Church itself—the cleansing, purifying, fertilising tide of the River of God, flows on for ever and ever.[1]

To give some idea of the effect of those words, let us recall the scene. It was at the Diocesan Conference of 1889, held in the large upstairs hall at St Peter's, Bishop Wearmouth. The hall was crowded. We waited for the arrival of our President, who had been at death's door. There was a tense silence that told how all hearts wondered how he would bear the great strain of meeting his Diocese again after his illness.

Suddenly we all rose to our feet. Carried up the stairs behind us at the back of the Hall, he came slowly walking up the aisle. The Conference stood listening to his weary footfall, and at length, lifted on to the platform, he gave us his Presidential Address, in which he seemed "dying and behold he lived".

---

[1] Address to the Diocesan Conference, October 1889.

Chapter VIII

THE BISHOP AND HIS CLERGY

TIME was, when a certain candidate seeking Holy Orders had to spend a solitary night in a hotel and go next day to the Ordination in the neighbouring Cathedral. He arrived at his Curacy after little more than a glimpse of his Bishop. It was not so in Durham, for Bishop Lightfoot was among the first to make the change from the old practice to what has now become the rule. The examination was always held three weeks or more before the Embertide, in order that, with minds freed from anxiety as to the result, the remaining days might be given to devotion, and further the Bishop invariably received all the candidates as his own guests for two full days' quiet spiritual preparation before their ordination. At the same time, the intellectual standard for candidates was steadily and continuously raised. For instance, during the last four years of Bishop Baring's episcopate, only one-fifth of those ordained were graduates of Oxford or Cambridge. In the first four years of Bishop Lightfoot's time, this proportion was increased to one-half, and that proportion was maintained to his death. Altogether he ordained 323 Deacons for the Diocese in the ten years of his episcopate.

Within a few weeks of his appointment, he made it known that his requirements in the case of non-graduate candidates for Holy Orders would be stricter than had hitherto been customary in the Durham Diocese. This created consternation in certain quarters. The Dean of Lichfield writes:

> I remember very well one morning in Cambridge meeting the Head of a Theological College who came up to Cambridge on behalf of several affected by the new rule, to see Dr Lightfoot, and (as he expressed it) to put him right, for he did not understand the situation. Two hours later I heard from Dr Lightfoot the account of the interview. It was his visitor who then understood the situation!

At least once a year the Ordination was held in one of the large towns of the Diocese. The effect of this policy may be estimated from a single episode. In September 1884 the Bishop ordained seven Deacons in the ancient church of St Hilda's, Hartlepool. Thirty years later one of these seven working in that town chanced to meet a working man who had been present and who vividly recalled the scene. He could not forget the intense solemnity and awe with which the Bishop pronounced the words of the Lord's Commission. "Man alive", he said, "I can hear him still with his '*Take thou authority*', in a voice that might have come out of a coalpit." This was rough, but it was true, revealing the deep and lasting impression made on this listener of the grave reality of Holy Orders.

Canon R. L. Ottley, Regius Professor of Moral and Pastoral Theology at Oxford, has kindly contributed the following recollections:

> The short period during which I was one of Bishop Lightfoot's examining Chaplains came to an end forty-four years ago! My reminiscences, therefore, are no longer so vivid as I could wish. I recollect, however, that, being very young and inexperienced, I was greatly encouraged in undertaking so responsible and difficult an office, partly by the warm welcome I received from my old college friend, Herbert Southwell, at that time a domestic chaplain at Auckland, and from my new colleague, the Rev. R. Appleton of Trinity; partly also by a letter

from an honoured friend at Oxford who pointed out the importance of any step which might lead to a closer connection between Oxford Churchmen and the great Cambridge school of which Bishop Light-foot was so conspicuous a representative. The Bishop himself, to whom I was an entire stranger, wrote with characteristic generosity in reply to some explanations on doctrinal points which it seemed right to offer before accepting from him so serious a trust: "I do not see anything in your further explanations", he said, "to which I should demur, though possibly I might use other forms of words.... I am quite sure from what you say, that these subjects, important as they may be in themselves, will not be allowed an undue prominence in your teaching to the detriment of the great doctrinal verities and ethical principles of the Gospel".

The Bishop evidently wished that his Chaplains should freely use every opportunity during the Ember-tides to give such spiritual help, guidance and comfort to the Ordinands as they might need at so solemn a turning point in their lives. All the arrangements at Auckland Castle were thoughtfully planned and admirably carried out by the domestic chaplains. The Bishop regarded us all alike, clergy and candidates, as his "sons", and in spite of his natural shyness and reserve, he managed to impart to the Embertide gatherings a really homelike atmosphere, which brought even to those who were troubled with fears and misgivings a spirit of confidence, hopefulness and quietness of mind. His own addresses, delivered in the beautiful and stately chapel on the eve of the Ordination, struck exactly the note of encouragement most needed by young men in such circumstances. They richly illustrate the grave reality, the sympathetic insight, the profound reverence and simplicity which were so conspicuous in the Bishop's dealings with his Ordinands. Not to enlarge, however, on the beauty and power of these unique addresses, I venture to quote one testimony which is perhaps typical of the spirit in which those ordained by the Bishop entered upon their difficult duties in the great industrial towns and pit-villages of the Durham Diocese. The memory of Arthur Fraser Sim, who offered himself for the work of the Universities' Mission in Central Africa, and eventually laid down his life in its service, is still cherished by those who knew and loved him at Cambridge and elsewhere. He wrote as follows from Sunderland, shortly after his ordination.

"The glamour of those happy days at Auckland, as well as at Durham, has not passed away yet, and I hope and think it never will.

It seems as if one had been taken into a different atmosphere. One's work seems so different. Quite a new power of self-surrender seems to have been given me, and what was drudgery before, seems a joy now. The only thing that mars the complete joy of the whole life is that one's powers are so limited. Days and weeks go by, and one seems to get so little done. And I am sorely tempted to envy certain gifts in others—the power to preach (it does seem to give help to others more almost than any gift); but above all, the power that some have of communing with God. . . . You see I need humility—to be content to use the few talents, and not to grumble because God has not given me more."

It should be added that there were occasions when the Bishop formed his own decided opinion of a man's spiritual capacity and fitness for the ministry, independently of examination results. "You did quite right in declining to pass him," he once said; "but I know the man and I shall ordain him nevertheless." I believe that in that particular case—and there may have been others—the Bishop was more than justified in his action by the man's subsequent career.

Some Oxford men who are still living recall with deep gratitude the Bishop's kindness in consenting to conduct the annual retreat for Graduates engaged in University and College work, which was held at Cuddesdon College. "I am a slow worker," he wrote in reply to our invitation, "and 'the time is short'. To do what you ask me to do—not well, but as well as I can do it—will take some time. If I were left to my own judgment, I should consider that my spare hours would be more wisely spent on work I could do better. Nevertheless, if you and your Oxford friends still desire that I should undertake this office, I feel that it would be wrong of me to decline again."

The addresses given on this occasion are printed in the volume of *Ordination Addresses* published after his death (1890). Those who attended the retreat can never forget the intense emotion with which the Bishop identified himself with St Peter's cry of self-abasement, "Depart from me, for I am a sinful man, O Lord". "Depart from me, and yet not so, O Lord. . . . Not so, Lord, for how can I endure to part from Thee. In Thy presence only is comfort, is strength, is hope, is light, is life!" Nor less impressive was the address on Phil. ii. 3, on the evils of ἐριθεία—"party spirit, the last infirmity of the religious man, the devoted and zealous follower of Christ, follower at least (at however great a distance) in His zeal and self-devotion, but not follower in His wide sympathy, in His large charity, in His concessive, indulgent moderation, His ἐπιείκεια, which is the direct negation of partisan zeal".

We who were allowed in any way to share his burden, and were associated with him in ministering to the spiritual needs of the young men who received from him their "great commission" have reason indeed to bless his memory. Our thoughts dwell, not so much on his intellectual gifts and his massive learning as on the example he gave us of unsparing and single-hearted devotion to God and to the work of His Kingdom. Fervent in spirit, great in humility, in zeal, in generosity, in wisdom, in patience, he so used his manifold gifts as to inspire and uplift all who came under his influence. Those whom he affectionately called his "dear sons" can thankfully echo some words of Augustine, speaking in the *Confessions* of his intercourse with Ambrose: *ad eum ducebar abs Te nesciens, ut per eum ad Te sciens ducerer.* And when we recall the text of the sermon which the Bishop preached at his enthronement in Durham Cathedral (Rev. xxii. 4: "They shall see His face") we cannot but feel that they represent the spirit, purpose and aim of his whole ministry. To him indeed life was the vision of the Unseen: *Vita hominis visio Dei.*

In the "obituary" of his Chaplain, the Rev. H. R. Banton, mentioned above, the Bishop writes:

I have had placed in my hands some extracts from a private Diary which he kept. Some of these extracts are too sacred, indeed too personal for publication, but I give this:

"Sunday. Mattins at 8.15. I felt calm and at peace. The day was a quiet gray, with a soft intermittent drizzle of rain. Just broke fast and nothing more. I had no fixed idea about fasting, but thought it better to err in too literal a following of the Apostles than too free a departure from them.

The service at South Church [the local name of the Parish Church of St Andrew, Auckland, where the Ordination was held] was full of a depth of peace and love to me, such as I have never known. The *Veni Creator* began the climax. My heart was full of an overpowering sense of my own unworthiness and Christ's deep love and trust in one who had done nothing but what deserved the withdrawal of love and trust; and at the actual imposition of hands the surge of mingled regrets and hopes, joys and fears, the sense of being at once infinitely humbled and exalted broke out *in lacrimas super ora surgentes et defluentes—Gaudebam, quia contristabar; contristabar, quia gaudebam."*

"A ministry so supported", comments the Bishop, "could not be otherwise than fruitful."

At the Ordination at St Andrew's, Auckland, on December 18th, 1881, Canon Body had preached from Rev. i. 16, "He had in his right hand seven stars". At lunch, afterwards, the Bishop in most affectionate terms reminded him that "seven Sons of the House" had been presented that day.

Another marked feature of the Bishop's interest in all his Clergy was the annual gathering of the Curates of the Diocese whom he invited to Auckland. The first invitation was issued in 1882 to those who had been ordained by the Bishop himself, when we remained at Auckland for two days. But later on it was extended to all the Curates, whether ordained by the Bishop himself or not, and then the pressure of accommodation became so great that the proceedings were necessarily limited to one day.

What red-letter days those annual gatherings were! To stand in worship in that glorious Chapel amid some 200 brother clergy, most of us under thirty years of age, with the Bishop himself among us was an inspiration. We had brilliant scholars and noted athletes. We had "unlearned and ignorant men". We were of all schools of thought with most varied upbringing. We should have differed in controversy; yet there, kneeling side by side, and receiving the Body and Blood of the Lord we felt we were one in Christ. As we spent the day together friendships grew, and the spirit of living unity and fellowship became as the air we breathed.

No wonder that ritual controversies were unheard of in the Diocese. The story goes that at the Newcastle Church

Congress, over which the Bishop presided, there came moments of keen tension, when feeling ran high and words were strong. Without uttering a word the Bishop slowly rose from his seat and raised his hand. At once the strife of tongues ceased. That scene is symbolic—the silent presence of such a Father in God with hand uplifted sent a thrill of brotherhood through the Con⁄gress, and thence this silent uniting influence spread throughout the Diocese. For example, a senior man, with Calvinistic traditions, found himself at home speaking in a parish where the ritual was utterly foreign to him, while on his side the Ritualist welcomed the Evangelical as a fellow⁄labourer.

At these gatherings of Curates we had such preachers as Canon A. J. Mason of Truro and Canterbury—and two successive Vicars of Leeds: Dr Jayne, later on Bishop of Chester, and Dr Talbot, Bishop of Rochester and then of Winchester.

But perhaps the Sermons which made the most lasting impressions were those of the Bishop himself, preached to Ordination Candidates and on St Peter's Day Gather⁄ings, some of which are fortunately preserved in the volume, *Ordination Addresses*, published by the Trustees of the Lightfoot Fund. To those who actually heard the addresses, these pages recall the living man. At times as he spoke his voice wavered and he was overwhelmed. But on he would go in spite of tears. This was no mere emotion—"sentimentality" was utterly alien to his character—but the great and humble man seemed to become suddenly conscious that the Living God was speaking through him to his hearers, and our spirits are even now revived as we read his words.

Many of the present generation have never heard of the

book and they will welcome extracts. They will see that, while his teaching fed the soul and strengthened resolve, his perfect simplicity revealed a new and telling style of preaching—deep truths in simple words, pithy sentences alive with meaning because they were the manifest transcript of his own experience, such as "Christ's crucifixion demands your crucifixion"—"Sympathy cures selfishness"—"Hopelessness is faithlessness".

Frequently, like a riveter, he would seize a glowing thought and with arm uplifted, suiting the action to the word, he would drive it home again and again.

For example "Depart from me" in the passage referred to by Canon Ottley:

...The marvellous bounty of God's grace dazzles and astounds our vision, and in our perplexity of heart the despairing, craving, forbidding, yearning cry is wrung from our lips "Depart from me, O Lord, for I am a sinful man".

"Depart from me, O Lord." I know it all now. I see my sin because I see Thy goodness. Yes, I have beheld Thy holiness, Thy purity, Thy truth, Thy grace, Thy power, Thy love, and I have been stunned with the contrast to self. The brightness of the light has deepened the blackness of the shade.

"Depart from me, O Lord." What can I have in common with Thee! I so selfish, so vile, so sinladen, with Thee so merciful, so righteous, so holy, so pure! In very deed Thy ways are not as my ways and Thy thoughts are not as my thoughts!

"Depart from me, O Lord." This fear of the Lord is indeed the beginning of wisdom. This consciousness of sin is the straight pathway to heaven. The saintliest of men have ever spoken and felt most strongly of their own sinfulness. The intensity of their language has provoked the sneers of the worldling. Has he not evidence here, on their own confession, that despite all their pretensions to holiness, they are no better than he? But they know, and he does not know, what sin means, for they know what God means. And therefore the despairing cry is wrung from their agony, "Depart from me, O Lord".

"Depart from me"; and yet not so, O Lord. Even while Peter is

speaking, his gestures belie his words. His lips implore Jesus despair-
ingly to depart, but his eyes and his hands entreat Him to stay. Not so,
Lord, for how can I endure to part from Thee? In Thy presence only
is comfort, is strength, is hope, is light, is life.

"Depart from me?" Nay: it is for the godless to say "Depart from
us, for we desire not the knowledge of God". It is for the unclean
spirits to rave against Thee, "Let us alone, Thou Jesus of Nazareth,
what have we to do with Thee?" But I, I have everything to do with
Thee. I am created in the image of God. I have a ray of the Divine
Light, a seed of the Divine Word, within me. And like seeks like.
Therefore, I yearn after Thee; therefore I am drawn towards Thee;
therefore I stretch out my hands to Thee over the wide chasm of sin
which yawns between us: Lord to whom shall we go? Thou hast the
words of eternal life. [1]

Dr Ottley also "remembers as illustrating all this" the
effect of the last paragraph, "Alas, brothers, I am ashamed
to tell you", in the following passage, in the opening
Address of the Cuddesdon series which discloses one
secret of his influence over us.

And how can I better make my apology before you than by adopting
the words of a true saint of God—one who had less—far less need of this
line of defence than I am conscious of having?

Thus writes Leighton to the clergy of his synod at Dunblane:
"Is it not brethren an unspeakable advantage beyond all the gainful
and honourable employments of the world, that the whole work of our
particular calling is a kind of living in heaven, and besides its tendency
to the saving the souls of others, is all along so proper and adapted to the
saving of our own?

'But you will possibly say, What does he himself that speaks these
things to us? Alas, I am ashamed to tell you. All I dare say is this.
I think I see the beauty of holiness, and am enamoured of it, though I
attain it not, and howsoever little I attain, would rather live and die in
the pursuit of it than in the pursuit, yea in the possession, and enjoyment,
though unpurified, of all the advantages that this world affords. And I
trust dear brethren you are of the same opinion, and have the same desire
and design, and follow it both more diligently and with better success.'

[1] *Ordination Addresses*, pp. 234–36.

'Alas,' brothers, 'I am ashamed to tell you.' And it is just the hope that this shame and humiliation, as I look back on the splendid opportunities of an academic teacher, and reflect on the poor use which I myself made of them, may give some force and edge to words which would otherwise be powerless—it is just the hope which gives me courage to address you. Do not press the question home. 'Alas, I am ashamed to tell you'".[1]

When Bishop Sandford of Tasmania came as his assistant, Bishop Lightfoot was able to tell him that there were more clergy working without stipend in Durham than in any Diocese in the country. This was the very greatest help in developing work. For example in two of the great towns he was able to place a man capable of laying the foundation of a future parish, so that the Church was first in the field instead of being last.

In one of these cases the rich man had offered to go as voluntary Curate to a town to be near his lifelong friend. The Bishop tested his self-sacrifice by asking him to go elsewhere to one of the hardest and most uninviting posts in the Diocese. A large and beautiful Church and vigorous parish are the results to-day of work begun by such self-sacrifice and devotion.

In the other case some older clergy objected to such a young man being appointed, and one went so far as to express his protest to the Bishop. "Would you have gone there", said the Bishop, "I had no stipend to offer?" The reply was "No," and the grumbling ceased.

Though inexperienced, and often single-handed, a young Curate so placed felt strong with the backing of the Bishop at every turn. One still living writes:

He was eager that I should take a post which he was anxious to fill. There were possible and probable difficulties and after a talk I said "I am not sure that I should care to go". "You're not going, you're

[1] Ibidem, pp. 217–18.

being sent", was his reply. "Then," I said, "when am I to go?" "Next week", and next week I went.

Another Curate offering himself for some extra-paro-chial work was being dealt with in a somewhat high-handed manner by a certain society. He jumped into the train and took the unpleasant letter to the Bishop. Suddenly the society found that instead of dealing as they liked with an unknown Curate, they were face to face with the Bishop of Durham. They were made to toe the line in no uncertain way, and the Curate was established in his new position. The young man, whom the Bishop thus befriended, did a work later on of similar nature, in a large and important centre amidst most tremendous difficulties, which has had far-reaching and lasting influence.

His absolute trust in his young men was remarkable. An ex-President of the University Boat Club working in the Diocese got a letter one day. "Can you find me a job in Durham, I'm sick of this quiet Country?" He wrote on the corner of the letter, "He weighs 12 stone and puts every ounce on his blade when he rows", and sent it to the Bishop. "Tell him to come", was the only reply. He came, and for more than forty years he has rowed his full weight in some of the roughest water in the Diocese.

But, while it was said (and sometimes with feeling) that the Bishop "believed in young men", he was scrupulously loyal to those who had spent their lives in the Diocese. His first appointments before he was consecrated were two senior men of opposite schools of thought whom he asked to serve as Honorary Chaplains, and it is significant that in the list of Honorary Canons whom he appointed all were working in the Diocese before he came, except a younger man who held a

Canonry for a time as a lecturer in Church History in the three Northern Dioceses.

A Rector told the Bishop he had a promising senior Curate, who after five years' service had been offered and refused a living in another Diocese. He suggested him for a vacant living that he might be kept in Durham. The Bishop replied that he had senior men whom he must consider first. He gave the living to a man who had special reasons for being sent there. The vacancy in a town thus created was filled by sending a man glad to go for the sake of his children's education. This vacated a benefice in the gift of the Rector who had written to the Bishop, who was thus able himself to promote his man, keep him in the Diocese, and retain him as a neighbour.

West Hartlepool is often quoted as an illustration of his masterly skill in marshalling his men. He found it at a very low ebb with only three churches, in none of which was an effective ministry. As soon as possible he put in a group of men who would compare well with any set of men in any town. And in an astonishingly short time the whole scene changed and it became a strong Church centre. Years later it was referred to as "holy ground" by a clergyman in the south who heard of the clergy it sent forth as missionaries: F. N. Eden and H. H. Dobinson from St James to C.M.S. on the Niger; Arthur F. Sim from St Aidan's to U.M.C.A. at Kota Kota; E. F. Every from St Paul's to South America; and W. F. Cosgrave from Christ Church to the Dublin University Mission in Chota Nagpur.

All these were from Lightfoot's "young men", to whom he had said:

...You must be conscious of a voice within you...in some way or other the prompting must be felt, the voice must be heard. 'Here is a work, God's work, to be done. And God wants *me*. God summons *me* to do it. I know my weakness; I know my inability; I know my ignorance, my inadequacy, my unworthiness in all respects; but notwithstanding this sense of feebleness, I will obey the summons. Notwithstanding it? Nay, by reason of it; for is not strength, God's strength, made perfect in weakness? I cannot bear to think of so many souls perishing for lack of food. I cannot bear to see so many sons of God estranged from their Father in Heaven. A ministry of reconciliation, of reconciliation—why, the very name draws me with an attractive power which I cannot resist.

Dost thou ask Lord, "whom shall I send? And who will go for us?" There is only one answer, "Here am I, send me".[1]

---

[1] *Ordination Addresses*, p. 49.

Chapter IX

THE BISHOP'S THANK-OFFERING

ST IGNATIUS THE MARTYR, SUNDERLAND

IN the autumn of 1887 the Bishop wrote to Canon Mathie, the Rector of Hendon, Sunderland, stating that at the close of his seven years' episcopate he was desirous to build a Church as a thank-offering, and it was most fitting that it should be in the most populous parish in the Diocese with its 30,000 inhabitants, chiefly work-ing men, who could not be expected to subscribe large sums.

By the autumn of 1889 the Church was nearing completion, and the Bishop chose, as its first Vicar, the Rev. Edgar Boddington, one of his "sons". 10,000 people were allotted to the new parish.

The architect of the new Church was Mr C. Hodgson Fowler, Cathedral Architect, who designed a handsome church in Early English style, somewhat severe, but full of quiet dignity. The pillars in the nave were by the Bishop's wish reminiscent of clustered columns in the Chapel at Auckland Castle.

Most appropriately the Church was dedicated to the memory of St Ignatius the Martyr, and the handsome stone reredos contains on either side of the Crucifixion figures of Bishops of East and West—Ignatius and Polycarp for the East, and Cuthbert and Aidan for the West. A noble Te Deum window above this reredos makes the east end the crowning glory of the Church.

The whole of the exterior to the summit of the fine

broach spire is of white ashlar stone brought from Edmundbyers quarries. There is a fine peal of eight bells, and Bishop Forrest Browne drew up a complete scheme for stained windows of historical interest throughout the Church. Those in the nave were founded on Bede's *Ecclesiastical History*, while those in the chancel illus-trated the life of Ignatius. The west window embodies the life of the founder from his schooldays under Dr Prince Lee to his death.

The Bishop, though in failing health, took the liveliest interest in the work, guiding negotiations of some delicacy in the early stages of the formation of the new parish. At a Saturday night Men's Bible Class here an old ex-Wesleyan offered fervent prayer for the new incumbent. "Bless, O Lord, the young man, bless him, O Lord, we think he'll do. We think he'll do." This vastly delighted the Bishop. He slyly remarked, "I like the record of a suspended judgment".

In the anxious spring of 1889 it was more than doubt-ful whether the Bishop's strength would rally. Yet in ill-ness he could not forget St Ignatius. As compline was read at his bedside his voice boomed out before the concluding prayer, "Pray for Boddington". And when the turn came for the better, the young Vicar received the following letter in the familiar writing:

My dear Son,—I hear on all sides you are overworking yourself. I charge you, should it even mean putting a notice on the Mission Room door that services will be discontinued for a time, that you at once take a brief rest. That you may realise how imperative is this charge, I need only add this is the first letter I have written "with my own hand" since my very, very serious illness.

Yours affectionately,

J. B. DUNELM.

By the mercy of God he recovered sufficiently to return from Bournemouth, which is thus recorded on the hand-some brass lectern given as a thank-offering:

> He was sick nigh unto death, but God had mercy on him, and on us also.

He was able to consecrate his gift himself on July 2nd, 1890, when he was surrounded in St Ignatius Church with a great host of surpliced clergy from all over the Diocese. He was wonderfully sustained to bear the strain of the very long Service of Consecration.

The preacher, most appropriately, was Dr Westcott. His text "From weakness were made strong", Heb. xi. 34, was used to gather up the stories of the ages—and the recovery of the Bishop—and the lesson of St Ignatius. Referring to the Bishop he said:

> Do you not feel that his influence has extended far beyond the limits of our own Communion, because he has recognised the breadth of his obligations and moved among you as the representative of the whole Diocese? Do you not feel that the forty-five houses of God, which have risen in answer to his appeal, the seventy "sons of his house", whom he has sent to minister to you, witness to a force gathered from old times, quickened but not created? Do you not feel that that unity, for which we all are longing, has been brought a little closer to us, when all Durham looks to him as the natural leader in every movement for education, for temperance, for social purity? I have a right to use a personal argument. He who wisely uses the resources of an institution is the interpreter, and, in some sense, the measure of its power. The great man is the sign of the great society.
>
> And for us to-day the largest thoughts must take a personal shape. I have just spoken of this building, most religious in its solemn dignity, as a memorial of an episcopate rich in abiding fruits, a memorial of sacrifices offered and blessed, of prayers made and answered. And it is in a true sense a living memorial. For there is, indeed (would that we did not forget it), between a gift and a bequest the whole difference of life. The benefactor lives in his gift. He himself works through it, and

he enjoys the fruits of its working. This Church of Ignatius places its giver's long-chosen literary labours, which he postponed to his appointed charge, in connexion with your services to Christ, in which he will find his great reward. It offers to you, by its unique dedication, the inspiring example of a new Saint. It has received no material relics, but its very stones are the witness of self-surrender. It holds no letters written in the dust (as in the ancient ritual) by the bishop's staff, but letters written by his love on the heart of him who will minister in it. It teaches you to look beyond England in order that you may feel your debt and your duty. It reminds you of the wide-spread glory of your spiritual ancestry, in which you reckon side by side an apostle of the far East and an apostle of the far West—Ignatius of Antioch and Columba of Hy. It discloses, if you study its memories, the secret of spiritual transfiguration, *from weakness were made strong*.[1]

Moved by the thought of all his generosity, his "sons" resolved to offer the Bishop £100 a year for three years toward the Curate Fund of the new Church. In acknowledging this he wrote:

SANDYKELD,
BOURNEMOUTH.
Christmas 1888.

My dear Auckland Sons,

I cannot forbear any longer, though the dictation of a letter is irksome to me, expressing to you, if not with my own pen, yet in my own words, my gratitude for your recent action in contributing towards the stipend of a Curate for St Ignatius, Hendon. The thought has relieved the pain of more than one wearisome night.

It is to me a matter of good augury that the Auckland Students are looking upon St Ignatius, Hendon, as, in a sense, a special charge, so long as it needs their aid. For some time the incumbent will have serious financial difficulties in organising the Parish, and such help and sympathy as you are giving him cannot fail to be most acceptable.

I entertain the hope that in the future the Auckland Students will regard this Church as a special centre of union, and meet from time to time to commemorate by solemn services our bond of brotherhood.

[1] *From Strength to Strength*: Three sermons by Bishop Westcott. Macmillan, 1890.

Asking the support of your prayers during this trying illness, and wishing you all every Christmas and New Year's blessing,

I am

Your very affectionate

J. B. DUNELM.

Our St Peter's Day reunion has been held there more than once.

The £100 a year payment was steadily maintained till after the War. Then it became evident that we could not indefinitely continue. So we began to reduce the sum handed to the parish by £10 a year; and the balance received in subscriptions was placed to an Endowment Fund which received special contributions, notably one of £100. In this way, with the help of the Ecclesiastical Commissioners, a permanent endowment has been secured and the Curate Fund finally wound up.

Bishop Westcott, as we have seen, continued the Brotherhood in the same spirit as our founder, and on St Peter's Day 1899 we offered to place a window in the Chapel at Auckland to commemorate his own ten years' episcopate. He gladly accepted, suggesting that we should unite our Thanksgiving with his own, and he made two conditions: (1) that the subject should be his predecessor's episcopate, and (2) that our subscriptions should be limited, that he himself might bear the bulk of the cost.

In writing to acknowledge our gift of fifty-five guineas, he wrote:

I took heart, as you know, to come to Durham because I believed that my lifelong friendship with my predecessor would enable me to sympathise with his methods of work and to win the confidence of those who had caught his spirit.

My hope has been more than fulfilled, and my great joy in the close of my work is to be assured that, by the blessing of God, you will maintain undiminished, for those who come after, that energy of love which has been my stay and inspiration through ten years of anxious yet happy labour.

No privilege can be greater than to be allowed to call myself with deep affection,

Your Father in God,

B. F. DUNELM.

AUCKLAND CASTLE,
March 27th, 1901

Two "Lightfoot Memorial Churches" were built in the Diocese: St Hilda's, Sunderland, and St Aidan's, Gateshead. The Norman Chapter House of the Cathedral was restored as the Diocesan Memorial to him.

Phot. Debenham & Gould

BISHOP LIGHTFOOT IN 1889

Chapter X

THE CLOSING DAYS

IN recognition of the completion of the ten years of his episcopate it was resolved in August 1888 to present the Bishop with his portrait and a pastoral staff. The proposal was met with enthusiasm all over the Diocese.

In view of the Bishop's illness the Committee decided to make the presentation on October 29th, 1889, before he left for the south.

A remarkable gathering met in Bishop Cosin's library on that October afternoon. The Lord Lieutenant (Lord Durham) presided. He explained to the Bishop that the staff could not be finished before the end of the year—but here it was "in its rough state just as it left the workman's shop, some of its parts put together temporarily for this occasion"—for a strong desire was felt to present it before the Bishop left for the south.

How Lord Durham felt may be judged from the following sentences:

I have in my possession—and I am proud of and shall always value it—a letter you addressed to me last year from Bournemouth. You were too feeble except to dictate that letter and append your signature to it, but I shall never forget that in that letter you expressed your belief that you might never again come among us, and the only regret, the only sorrow that the idea of death had for you, was that you would be unable to work as hard as you had formerly done. Now that we have you with us again, I can assure you, in the name of all classes, of all sects, and of all denominations in this county, that we hope you may long live to resume and fulfil the work among us. But had you never been able again to do any of this work, I can assure you we are proud of the work you have done for us in the past, and we shall ever remember with pride the noble record of your life among us.

The Lord Lieutenant then handed to the Bishop the pastoral staff.

Lord Londonderry and others having spoken, the Bishop rose and was received with great warmth. He said:

This is indeed a happy moment for me. I should have felt no common satisfaction if the purpose of our gathering had been simply the presentation of the pastoral staff, which, I can see already in its present unfinished state, will do honour to your intention and will be a most valuable heirloom of the See of Durham after my death. But I cannot fail to remember to-day that there is another source of gratification to me; it is the reception of your kindly welcome, now that it has pleased God to recover me, at least in a partial measure, in answer to your prayers.

．　　　．　　　．　　　．　　　．　　　．　　　．

May I say something about the double present which this meeting represents? Mention has already been made of the portrait. I am glad for more reasons than one that it is nearly completed. I hope that the last sitting is over—I am no judge whatever whether it is a good likeness. My friends who have seen it say that it is. But of one thing I am sure, that as a work of art it will be no discredit either to Mr Richmond's great reputation, or to your kindly intentions.

And now just a word or two with regard to the presentation of this day.

Some years ago, when I was comparatively new to the Diocese, it was suggested to me that some such gift might be made—I said then I thought it was somewhat premature. The Diocese could not be supposed to understand me, and it might possibly give rise to wrong impressions. I have no fear of that kind to-day. If I have not proved by my words and deeds in these ten years that I have not been, and never intend to be, the Bishop of a party, but the Bishop of the diocese; I am afraid that nothing henceforward which I could say or do would correct the impression. But since those times there has been a great change in public opinion about these matters. I recollect a few years ago—three or four years ago—I went down to Wells to preach in the

Cathedral there. I found that my venerable friend, the Bishop of Bath and Wells (Lord Arthur Hervey) was preceded by a pastoral staff, and that this pastoral staff was carried by a respected Oxford professor. Now the Bishop of Bath and Wells, as everybody will allow, is the very type of moderation. And I think it would have very much astonished Professor Gandell[1] if he had been called in any sense, an extreme man. In fact, from that time forward it became to me rather a humorous idea that there was any party notion attached to the pastoral staff.

I have had in my possession, since I became Bishop, a symbol of another kind—a rather handsome mace—which I have used, and used without scruple from time to time. Now a mace is a very good thing. I daresay you will recollect that in the Bayeux tapestry a certain famous prelate, Odo, the half brother of the Conqueror, is represented as bearing a mace. It is at the battle of Hastings. It was considered not etiquette that a Bishop should shed blood, he must not unsheath his sword, but there was no harm in his belabouring the brains of the poor Saxons with his mace. And accordingly he is represented, by those who were intimately acquainted with him, in the Bayeux tapestry, as doing this very thing.

Now I do not suppose that you are under any apprehension that I should use the mace in this way. Whatever my own bloodthirsty feelings might lead me to do in the case of recalcitrant clergy or laity, I am afraid public opinion would be too strong for me.

But does not the mace suggest rather civil and political office than spiritual and ecclesiastical? The Palatinate had its glories, but thank God it is over. I cannot forget that the only predecessor who bore my own name in the long line of Bishops of Durham—Bishop Butler, the most humble and modest of all prelates, and the least disposed to earthly splendours—when he became Bishop of Durham made it a condition that the Lord Lieutenancy should not be separated from the episcopate. I do not blame him for doing so. He considered himself the champion of the rights of the See, for if he was not, who else would be? But I am most thankful that at the next vacancy it passed out of episcopal hands.

...I cannot help thinking that the pastoral staff is a much more suitable symbol of office for a Bishop than a mace. For what does a pastoral staff mean? The Christian minister, whatever else he is—and

[1] Laudian Professor of Arabic at Oxford. Examining Chaplain to the Bishop of Bath and Wells. Canon Residentiary of Wells Cathedral.

I shall not enter upon controversial questions—is, before all things, a pastor, a shepherd. Our Lord Himself takes to Himself the title of Chief Shepherd. This is the distinguishing mark which separates the Christian ministry from the heathen priesthood, and even from the Jewish priesthood. The heathen priests were slaughterers of victims. The Jewish priests, though they had other functions, yet had this as their chief work: the pastoral office was not necessarily attached to the Jewish priest. David was a Pastor: the Prophets were Pastors. But the priests need not necessarily have been so, though on occasions they were, when they had the gift. It is, therefore, a distinctly Christian symbol which you are placing in my hands to-day.

I would add also that the decorations of which you can hardly form any conception at present, will remind me of the best and most spiritual days in the history of the Northumbrian See. There will be represented there Aidan, Hilda, Bede, and others—the great makers, not only of the Church of England, but likewise of the polity and civilisation of England. I shall have these always before me as this staff is borne before me, bright examples of the past, which I can only attempt to follow at a long distance.

For all these lessons, I have to thank you to-day, and I pray that God may send His blessing upon you all, that you may bear tenderly with your Bishop, if the state of his health does not allow him to do such active service physically as he did before, and that the administration of this great Diocese may notwithstanding, as by your aid I trust it will, go on as efficiently and successfully as hitherto.

This report, from the record printed at the time[1], has been given at some length because it was the Bishop's last utterance and public appearance in the Diocese. And also because he revealed almost unconsciously the secret of his habitual caution and reserve, not due to natural shyness, but because of his strict avoidance of any suspicion of party bias. And he tells us his own estimate of the principles of his episcopate; the essentially spiritual character of a Bishop's office and work; the inspiration of

[1] *Presentation of a Pastoral Staff to the Bishop of Durham.* Durham: Andrews and Co., 1890.

a great Church heritage; as well as his gratitude for the welcome by the whole Diocese there gathered after his return from his serious illness.

Shortly after, he went to Bournemouth, and died less than eight weeks later on St Thomas' Day, December 21st, 1889.

The following extracts from different brethren tell their own story. The first two belong to the early stages of his illness, the others to the last.

§ 1

My most sacred experience was when I went to him at Bournemouth in his extreme illness. The heart trouble was causing complications frequently requiring attention. He was much distressed, but not with the prospect of death, which indeed was not remote. I remember his saying once, as I sat at his bedside, "What distresses me is the thought that this illness might produce some unreality of mind, and that I should say things that are untrue".

§ 2

Once during that visit at Bournemouth, I was going to give the Sacrament to a young priest dying of consumption. The Bishop knew —he rose, and resting on his hands, said with difficulty, "Tell him to be of good cheer. Tell him it is the message of one who has just looked death close in the face himself".

§ 3

On Sunday, December 15th, the Bishop seemed not quite so well and the falling off continued on Monday the 16th. He kept on at his literary work, however, with his usual keen interest and tenacity. On Tuesday about bedtime he was attacked with faintness and became exceeding weak and ill. Harmer, and his butler Wakefield, helped him with considerable difficulty to bed. Next morning he was able to leave his room, but did very little work. His passion for work, however, never left him, and even during the doctor's leaving the room for a moment, a few words were added to the sentence in his Clement of Rome, which proved to be the last words he wrote.[1]

§ 4

I arrived on Thursday December 19 and found him evidently drifting into a state of unconsciousness with occasional intervals when he would open his eyes. When I talked of the Ordination candidates who would be assembling,[2] he took little notice and evidently had not the power to think much of such things.

A Christmas card sent him by the wife of his oldest Chaplain, he took in his hand and looked at carefully, and said "Please thank her". When I drew his attention to the verse and said she had chosen that because she thought he would like it, he read it very carefully and slowly and smiled, and said "Yes, mind you thank her". The verse was Romans viii, part of 38 and 39, "I am persuaded that neither death, nor life...nor things present, nor things to come,...shall be able to separate us from the love of God which is in Christ Jesus our Lord".

This was his last effort of intelligent attention, and these words the last on which his eyes rested.

.   .   .   .

[1] We may be forgiven if our filial affection recalls in connection with this moving story the description of the last moments of the great Northumbrian saint and scholar given by Bishop Lightfoot in *Leaders in the Northern Church* (p. 89): "A man past the middle of life lay on his death-bed, surrounded by his disciples. They were sorrowing, says a bystander who relates the incident, at the thought that they should see his face no more in this life. A youth was taking down some words from the master's lips. 'One chapter still remains', said the lad, 'of the book which thou hast dictated; and yet it seems troublesome to ask more of thee.' 'It is not troublesome,' said the dying man, 'get out thy pen and prepare, and write quickly.' So the hours went on. At intervals he conversed with his scholars; then again he dictated. At length his amanuensis turned to him; 'Beloved master, one sentence only remains to be written.' 'Good,' he replied, 'write it.' After a short pause the boy told him that it was written. 'Good,' said he, 'it is finished; thou hast said truly.' And in a few moments more he gave up his soul to God, with his last breath chanting the doxology, familiar to him, as to us".

[2] Bishop Sandford, the assistant Bishop, and a large company of Ordination candidates were assembled at Auckland Castle on Saturday, St Thomas' Day, for the Ordination next morning. But the news of the Bishop's death received in the evening cancelled Bishop Sandford's commission, so no Ordination could take place. Among the candidates thus delayed were two Auckland Brothers, who are now English Bishops.

The grey old walls of Durham Cathedral can seldom have witnessed a more wonderful service than the funeral of Bishop Lightfoot on Friday, December 27th, 1889. The great church was filled from end to end with a congregation gathered from all classes and all corners of the Diocese and of England. Peers and pitmen, Churchmen and Dissenters, representatives of Cambridge University and St Paul's Cathedral were all brought together by a common sorrow, and all upheld by one triumphant faith.

The coffin which had rested overnight at a spot in "the Nine Altars" (still marked by a small brass cross on the floor) was borne by us "Sons of the House" in our surplices. By relays of eight at a time the very heavy burden was borne along the south aisle, and up the nave till it rested just below the great throne of the Bishop. It was preceded all the way by his Chaplain, the Rev. E. A. Welch, carrying the unfinished silver pastoral staff draped in crape.

A lifetime has passed since that dark day, yet still we recall the fellowship of loss, upheld by the faith and hope that found expression in the music and in fervent prayers.

The service ended, we bore all that could die of our master along the nave again, and through the cloister to the Deanery door, where his old coachman and his own horses were ready to take the hearse to Bishop Auckland, through pit villages filled with mourners.

A special train meanwhile took many to Auckland.

And there in the dimly lit Chapel we "Sons" stood in a double row round the open grave that was made before the sanctuary steps.

Archbishop Thomson of York stood at the "north end". Archbishop Benson of Canterbury stood at the step at the foot of the grave, and, a sad figure in his black coat, Dr Westcott stood at the head. Thus the three schoolfellows were together, Benson reading the commit, tal, and Westcott casting earth to earth. Standing on the brink of Eternity we learned that love is stronger than death.

On that dark afternoon in December 1889 Rolt and I went out after the funeral on to the sunless north terrace with a sense of gloom unspeakable. I had then no home of my own, and now our Father in God was taken from us, and the Diocesan Home (we supposed) had come to an end. No one not of Auckland could understand, any more than we could explain, what the tie was, or how it became so quickly knit. Looking back I think it was not because the Bishop was so good to us, or did many things for us, but because he *wanted* us, as a father wants his sons.

The black marble slab over the Bishop's grave, a "Memorial Offering of the Auckland Students", was worked out by Mr G. Hodgson Fowler, in conjunction with Bishop Westcott, who wrote the inscription, as follows:

HIC REQUIESCIT IN PACE JOSEPHUS BARBER LIGHTFOOT EPISCOPUS DUNELMENSIS ORATOR SCRIPTOR MAGISTER DOCTRINA ELOQUENTIA CANDORE PAENE PROPRIO FIDEM CHRISTI VINDICAVIT ECCLESIAE ORIGINES ILLUSTRAVIT INGENIO ET MORIBUS SUOS SIBI DEVINXIT POS-TEROS BENEFICIIS NATUS MDCCCXXVIII OBIIT MDCCCLXXXIX.

The lettering for this inscription was copied from the Lindisfarne Gospels.

The cross, which extends the whole length of the slab, is copied from the Saxon tombstone in Kirkdale Church, one of the few stones with an inscription in Runic characters. Many years ago these runes, then visible, were deciphered as "Cyning (King) Aethelwald". This is probably the tomb of Aethelwald, or Oidilwald, son of Oswald, King of Deira.

The two scrolls on either side of the cross are modelled from scrolls on fragments of shafts of Christian crosses, and the Alpha and Omega at the head are designed from the letters on a slab from the Hartlepool nuns' cemetery of St Hilda's day.

The Greek inscription

ΑΝΔΡΙΖΕΣΘΕ ΚΡΑΤΑΙΟΤΣΘΕ

written beneath his photograph among the Revisers of the New Testament in Dr Westcott's Album, is in letters taken from Celtic manuscripts.

Thus the slab gathers up in itself the history of the beginnings of Christianity in the North of England.

IN THE LEARNED WORLD

For ten years after his Episcopal consecration he continued to add to the pile of his Theological achievements. Had he survived for another twenty years it is difficult to believe that he would not have gone on toiling as fruitfully and brilliantly.... There he sat to the instant of his death, analysing, comparing, adjudicating....

He neither forgot the Bishop in the Scholar, nor the Scholar in the Bishop.

"The Times" Obituary, December 24, 1889.

Chapter XI

THE SCHOLAR STILL AT WORK

(a) *Bishop Lightfoot's Literary Work at Durham*[1]

BY THE REV. H. E. SAVAGE

NOT many generations have passed since a Bishopric was regarded as the natural goal of a scholar's life, in which, with much leisure and a few occasional routine duties, he might devote himself almost exclusively to his studies. But those days have happily passed away, and the present danger is rather that in the demand for practical men of business capacity, the claims of scholarship to be duly represented in the highest posts of the Church should be passed over. The calls upon a Bishop's time and energies are simply endless: the enormous growth of population during the past twenty or thirty years in most of the English Dioceses has by no means been met by a few tardy subdivisions; and the administrator of a large Diocese has his hands so full that it seems an impossibility for him to save any time for literary work. Every parish demands individual attention, and looks for at least occasional personal visits; Confirmations must be multiplied until they are held annually within reach of every parish; there is not a Church Society but looks to the Bishop to champion its cause in various centres; conferences, committees, organisations, gatherings of special bodies, etc., tend to increase on every side; while the daily post alone brings in enough work to employ the time of one man. In such a life as this, how

[1] Reprinted, by permission, from *The Classical Review*, February, 1890.

is it possible for a Bishop, however gifted, to secure any leisure for literary work?

It was such considerations as these that aroused a serious anxiety in every quarter, when the announcement appeared in the newspapers on January 28th, 1879, that Professor Lightfoot had accepted the See of Durham in succession to Dr Baring. With regard to the episcopal appointment, as such, the news was greeted with uni-versal satisfaction; but it was felt that the price would be altogether too great to pay for a powerful administrator in the Church if Dr Lightfoot's new responsibilities should prevent him from giving to the world any more of the eagerly expected results of his life-work on the writers of the New Testament and the Apostolic Fathers. A scholar of less note, it was urged, might well be found to organise and guide even such a great and difficult Diocese as that of Durham; but no one could fill Dr Lightfoot's place as a teacher and an expositor.

In the three months which intervened between his appointment and his consecration, while he was still at Cambridge, letters kept continually pouring in upon the Bishop-elect from all manner of correspondents imploring him to find time in some way or another to continue his literary labours; and Dr Westcott's sermon at the conse-cration of his friend in Westminster Abbey, in which he sketched the ideal of a Bishop's work, contained an earnest plea for patient thought and study and wise counsel on deeper subjects than mere diocesan detail or development. To one and all of these appeals the Bishop himself returned one steadfast answer; "he had not accepted the oversight of the Diocese to neglect its duties. Experience would show, but he would not venture to predict, whether any time would be left him to continue his literary work ".

Accordingly from his first entering on his new sphere he devoted himself unflinchingly to the administration of his Diocese; and frequently for weeks or even months at a time he found it impossible in the pressure of other work to secure any leisure for literary production. While however throughout his episcopate his Diocese held the first and paramount position in Bishop Lightfoot's thought and energy, he consistently kept before him as only a secondary responsibility the urgent claim which rested upon him as a scholar and a theologian to strive earnestly to finish the work which he had undertaken before he became a Bishop. It was this constant sense of a great duty incumbent upon him that led him to devote every leisure hour that could be spared from diocesan work to the prosecution of his literary labours.

It is not an easy matter to point to any definite time or occasion which the Bishop was able regularly to secure for his books in the midst of his busy life at Auckland Castle. In the earlier years of his life there, his habit was to rise very early in the morning, and lighting his own fire (which had been laid ready for him overnight) to make sure of two or three hours' quiet work in his bedroom before breakfast. But after a few years, when the terrible strain that pressed upon him began to tell upon his health, he reluctantly abandoned this plan as anything like a general rule.

When his constant engagements took him from home, he would sacrifice any personal convenience to return before night, or at least very early the following morning, in order to save as much time as possible. But even so the days at Auckland were seriously broken into. After breakfast he went through his letters with his Chaplains, reserving a certain number to answer with his own hand, amongst which were the numerous communications he constantly received from scholars in all parts of Europe. The preparation of sermons, speeches, charges, etc., necessarily occupied a great deal of attention. And though the position of Bishop Auckland saved him from a large number of the inconsiderate callers who, had he lived at Durham, would have occupied his time about matters that could have been dealt with as well by post, still there were not a few to whom an interview was really important, and who accordingly found their way to Auckland Castle. But with all these interruptions the last hour or two of the morning not infrequently found the Bishop engaged with his literary work, and he was often able to keep the greater part of the evening for it. Unfortunately too he would day after day restrict his exercise to a short stroll in his park, and then return to his work for the rest of the afternoon. For a man who had been used to a considerable amount of walking, this loss of fresh air and exercise was a serious strain upon his health.

The habit which the Bishop had formed of turning to his books at every available opportunity, however short, was exemplified even in the smallest details. Thus on his constant railway journeys, or in his long drives to the outlying villages of his Diocese, he always had with him as his constant companion a bag (familiarly known as "the Pandect"), in which were ready to his hand books, literary periodicals, proof-sheets, etc., for reference at any spare moment.

There was however one great opportunity for un-interrupted work open to the Bishop, which he was not slow to seize. When August came round, and he was able to get away for a summer holiday, he would carry off his books to some retired spot—generally in Scotland, and by preference to Braemar, where the bracing air and the quiet enabled him to work freely—and there he would abandon himself once more to a student's life. His dio׳ cesan correspondence followed him even there, but it did not reach him until midday, and the mornings and most of the evenings were kept sacred for literary work. It was during these holidays that a great part of his introduction to the *Ignatian Epistles* was written.

In the great bulk of his literary work Bishop Lightfoot depended entirely on his own labours. He never em׳ ployed an amanuensis; he rarely allowed anyone else even to verify his references. The only relief which he would accept was the almost mechanical correction of the proof׳sheets of the new editions, as they were called for, of his *Epistles of St Paul*. But latterly he entrusted more and more of his editing work to his Chaplain, the Rev. J. R. Harmer, who had prepared the indices for the edition of *St Ignatius*. In passing the sheets of his books through the press the Bishop spared no pains to ensure completeness in every detail; thus, for instance, one sheet of *Ignatius* was kept back for months to enable him to add if possible an English rendering which would pre׳ serve the play upon words in κακοδαίμων in the Antio׳ chene Acts of Martyrdom of St Ignatius (§ 11).

One great secret of the Bishop's being able to produce such a monument of learning and research as his *Ignatius* in the midst of an exceptionally active episcopate was the unique store of knowledge which he brought with him from Cambridge, and the remarkable accuracy of memory which enabled him to apply it readily. Page

after page was written *currente calamo* with few or no books
of reference at hand, and with only a "ver." here and
there in the margin where future verification was required.
He also had in a marked degree the power of again
taking up the thread of his work after an interruption
without a moment's hesitation. The thought of his complete and minute command of the whole range of the first
three centuries excites a keen regret that the pressure of
other business in the first instance, and afterwards the
state of his health, should have prevented him from
carrying out his original project, of writing a full historical introduction to his articles on "Supernatural
Religion" before re-issuing them in book form.

It would however be an inaccuracy to imply that all
the Bishop's interest and researches were confined solely to
the period of the Early Fathers. Apart from the various
topics of general and current interest which engaged his
attention, he was a thorough enthusiast and expert on the
subject of English Church history and antiquities, especially with regard to the unique heritage of his own
Diocese. He was among the first to claim for the Northumbrian mission of the seventh century its true position
in the evangelisation of England; and he was familiar
with every detail of the ecclesiastical antiquities of Durham
and Northumberland.

Auckland Castle came into his hands with few or no
relics of the See: he left it a monument of the history of all
his great predecessors from the days of Aidan himself.
Stained glass windows, shields, episcopal seals, portraits,
books, personal relics—such as the one faulty inscription
of Butler, or the desk of Cosin—all tell the story of the
past. In the summer of 1886 he began to prepare a monograph on the history of Auckland Castle, at which he

continued to work to the end as occasion offered.[1] His sermons on the North-Country Saints, preached at various churches dedicated in their names, will form a series[2] which in point of Early English Church history will carry far more than a merely temporary or local interest. The Bishop himself intended to publish these in a collected form when he had completed the whole cycle, according to the plan he had laid down for himself.

When Dr Lightfoot was appointed to Durham in 1879 there was some hope that he might be able to continue at intervals to give to the Northern University some of the lectures on the Greek Testament which had made him so famous as a teacher at Cambridge. His official position as Visitor of the University and Patron of the Canonries, with which two of its Professorships are endowed, seemed to give a certain ground for asking this of him. On more than one occasion during the first two years of his residence in the north he was urged to under-take such a course of lectures. But nothing would induce him to accede to this request. He felt that his hands were more than full of work in other directions, while the teaching staff of the University was amply sufficient for its needs. His interest however in the University never flagged, and it found a practical expression in the founda-tion by him in 1882 of the De Bury Scholarship for students who intend to take Holy Orders in the Diocese of Durham.

In his own home at Auckland Castle he gathered round him a band of graduates of the older Universities, who were reading with a view to taking Holy Orders in his Diocese. The teaching of these students was entrusted

---

[1] *Historical Essays.* Macmillan, 1895.
[2] *Leaders in the Northern Church.* Macmillan, 1895.

chiefly to the resident Chaplains, of whom there were always two on account of this special work. The Bishop himself occasionally gave them a course of Greek Testa-ment lectures, and the general direction of their studies rested with him: but more than this he was unable to do. Altogether, in the ten years eighty of these students have been trained at Auckland.

The one impression left upon the minds of all who knew Bishop Lightfoot, on a review of his ten years' episcopate, must always be that of a Father of the Church, who set himself to rule over his diocese with conspicuous devotion, judgment and ability; whose power of work seemed to be without limit, whose liberality was without stint; the motto of whose life was to spend and be spent for those to whom, as he himself expressed it on the day of his enthronement at Durham, he had given himself wholly for better or worse. And when to all his other labours was added the strain of the Lambeth Conference of 1888, in which he bore no small part, it was the last burden which hopelessly broke down his already over-taxed strength. In the midst of a life of such ceaseless and varied activity, it was only by the stern exercise of his inflexible will, and a steadfast and self-denying earnest-ness of purpose, that he was able in any degree to con-tinue his literary labours.

H. E. S. (1890)

(b) *The Bishop in his Study*

BY BISHOP HARMER

Throughout his residence at Auckland Castle Dr Light-foot had the continuous assistance of two domestic Chaplains. He had brought with him from Cambridge George Rodney Eden (till lately Bishop of Wakefield) and Henry Edwin Savage (now Dean of Lichfield); and his delight was great to find that as the son of a leading clergyman in his Diocese (Canon Eden, Rector of Sedgefield) Eden was thoroughly acquainted with the Diocese of Durham from end to end, knew many of its principal residents both in Durham and Northumberland and could arrange the Bishop's confirmation tours and other visits with an expert knowledge of the neigh-bourhood. This helped the Bishop greatly to become acquainted with his Diocese from the first.

Over and above the ordinary duties which fall to a Bishop's domestic Chaplain, such as writing letters, arranging interviews, organising his confirmation tours and the like, as well as accompanying the Bishop on his journeys when required to do so, the two resident Chap-lains at Auckland Castle were entrusted practically with the management of a large domestic establishment, in-cluding the social gatherings, and with the general supervision of the studies of the Auckland students, "the Sons of the House".

As one of this Brotherhood before my appointment to be a domestic Chaplain early in 1884, I came to my new office with a reverent acquaintance with the Bishop's character, his extraordinary power of work, his boundless trust in others, his simplicity of life, and his power of throwing off at a moment's notice all cares, whether diocesan or literary, and entering with an almost boyish spirit of detachment into the doings of the group of young men around him. He looked to them to provide him with the relaxation which he required from the strain of official life.

My duties began at a time when much which the Bishop had set himself to do at the commencement of his episcopate had been accomplished. It is evident that from the first he had kept steadily in view his cherished intention to complete, if possible, his unfinished literary work. But before he could find time for this he had to clear himself from three preliminary obligations—his work as a Reviser of the New Testament, the division of the Diocese of Durham, and the re-organisation of the diocesan machinery. Step by step he accomplished his aim. When, in the autumn of 1881 he presided at the Church Congress held at Newcastle, the Revised Version of the New Testament had just been published, and his absorbing work as a prominent Reviser had come to an end. The creation of the Diocese of Newcastle was also well in sight, and was happily accomplished in the following year. Relieved thereby of spiritual responsibility for Northumberland, the Bishop had set to work to organise in the completest manner what remained under his care, the historic county of Durham with its teeming population of coal miners. Durham presented itself to him as a strange contrast between the past glories of the old Prince Bishops, holding sway far North of the Tyne (of which only the emblems still remained—the sword crossed with the crozier and the mitre encircled with the ducal coronet)—and the overwhelming spiritual needs of the masses of workers flung upon the old county of

Durham by the recent sudden industrial expansion. The now familiar equipment of a modern diocese was then almost unknown. Bishop Lightfoot at once saw the magnitude of the effort needed to meet new conditions, and had thrown himself into it with characteristic courage and energy. In this reconstruction he had the very able help of Archdeacon Watkins, a most loyal friend and a most alert and capable organiser. The completeness of this new organisation is evident to all who have studied the Bishop's Primary Charge. All was done to concentrate the administrative duties of the Bishop regardless of the strain upon himself. Meetings of the principal diocesan societies were held in Durham at fixed days in each month, crowded together with an economy of time which must have taxed his powers as chairman. From the outset his confirmations had been arranged on a system of grouped parishes under alternate years, and so ordered that with much physical and mental exertion the Bishop carried them out for the most part single-handed in the early months of each year.

In all this we can see the Bishop's determination that without abating one jot of his episcopal duties, he should reserve for himself, at whatever cost, time for literary work at Auckland Castle.

In the remarkable appreciation of Dr Lightfoot's life and character which appeared anonymously in the *Quarterly Review* of January 1893, and has been since published separately (Macmillan, 1894), attention is drawn to the conflict between the "manifold responsi-bilities of the See of Durham" and the completion of the Bishop's monumental work on the Ignatian Epistles which was published in 1885, a year after I commenced my duties. "For weeks, and sometimes for months together", the Bishop tells us in his preface, "I have not found time to write a single line."

But with the organisation of the Diocese completed, the parishes visited one by one, and the clergy and principal laity personally known, he now felt himself free to devote more and more time to the conclusion of his great theological undertaking.

I had special opportunities of watching him as he sat in the inner study at Auckland Castle, writing at the desk presented to him by Trinity College, Cambridge, concentrating his attention more and more upon the achievement of "the *magnum opus* of his patristic studies and indeed of his life". His method, both at Cambridge and at Auckland Castle, was to work alone. As stated already by the Dean of Lichfield, his habit was to rise in the early morning before any member of the household, light his own fire and do some hours of work before breakfast-time, which was at a quarter to eight. If there was no diocesan engagement to interrupt him, he would snatch every possible moment (broken only by a short walk in the Park) in a day which for him did not end till the rest of the household were in bed. Except a few letters of importance, which he reserved for answers in his own hand, he passed on his diocesan and general correspondence to his Chaplains, merely indicating in the briefest manner the line which the answer should take.

On the other hand, his literary correspondence he conducted himself entirely. This correspondence was very considerable, for he was constantly exchanging letters with theological professors, librarians and patristic scholars of European eminence. He preferred to obtain what he needed in writing rather than by interviews or visits abroad. It was to him a more effective method. He possessed a wonderful memory for finding and bringing together at the proper moment all the material he required. He did not accumulate this material in notebooks compiled over long periods of time. In his working copies of Irenæus and Eusebius are to be found on the flyleaves pencil notes with brief headings and references to the pages. I have also seen a small papercovered indexed notebook in which references to articles in foreign theological reviews were recorded under their subjects. Possessed of an excellent library, especially strong in periodical literature in several languages, he had an almost intuitive perception of the place where material on any given subject could be found. He would then read up all the necessary authorities, sit down and write out his conclusions (whether essay, excursus or important paragraph), and send the result straight off to the press to be set up in type, just as it was. Once when I suggested a fair copy because the corrections, insertions and transpositions must add to the difficulty of setting up his material in type, his reply was: "No—send it up just as it is. It means that the Pitt Press will hand it over to their best compositor". The Bishop's habit of trusting to his memory at the moment is further illustrated by his unpublished notes on Pauline Epistles, which after his death came into my hands. They are of the most meagre description, and must have been expanded at the moment of their delivery as professorial lectures. Indeed notes taken by diligent students and kindly lent to me years after witness to this habit of amplification. The originals remained untouched since his Cambridge days.

The Bishop's knowledge of languages was very extensive. He said to me once in the simplest manner: "Does it not sometimes happen to you that when you have read a book you forget in what language it is written?" To him I suppose that would be true in at least seven languages (English, French, German, Italian, Spanish, Latin and Greek). And he had a consider, able, or at least a working, knowledge of several others, Hebrew of course, and Syriac, and Arabic and Ethiopic; moreover he was not unacquainted with Armenian (see *Supernatural Religion*, p. 287 note); while Dr Scrivener in his *Introduction to the Textual Criticism of the New Testa, ment*, singles him out by name as one of the three or four English scholars of his day thoroughly acquainted with the Coptic dialects. He was deeply interested in all Latin and Greek inscriptions, and I remember that when he visited the catacombs at Rome with Dr Nevin, the American Chaplain, our Italian guide blew out the candles in the hands of half our party, for fear we should be plunged into darkness, if we had no reserve of lights, so difficult was it to keep the Bishop from deciphering inscriptions, as he passed along.

The importance which he attached to ancient in, scriptions as illustrating Apostolic and sub,Apostolic literature is evident in all his published works; and I recall the great pleasure it gave him to receive for a short visit to Auckland Castle Professor Ramsay as he then was, afterwards Sir William Ramsay, fresh from his important discoveries in Asia Minor, among which was the famous Abercius inscription (see Lightfoot, *Ignatius*, I, pp. 478 ff.) witnessing to the unity of the Christian faith in the second century. This gave the Bishop particular delight.

My own very subordinate contribution to the Bishop's literary work consisted mainly in joining with others in correcting his proof,sheets, in looking up and verifying quotations, in collating one or two manuscripts and in indexing the volumes at the proper moment. He had a wonderful trust in others, and would generally accept results done by them just as they were. In the single volume edition of *The Apostolic Fathers*, which he was very anxious should be published, the part which I was permitted to contribute was supervised by him.

His power of detachment and concentration was extra-ordinary. I have seen him break off from an incomplete sentence for a momentous interview with one of his clergy, give him his undivided and sympathetic attention, followed by the wisest counsel and a final decision, and almost before the door was closed upon his visitor become once more absorbed in his literary work. His strength of will was such that frequently he would continue writing until the pen faltered in his hand and he fell asleep at his desk. Those who were privileged to minister to him in his last illness at Bournemouth, when, conscious of failing powers, he was determined to prepare for the press the last sheets of his larger edition of *Clement of Rome*, can recall a visit paid by his doctor (Dr Roberts Thomson) on the Tuesday before his death when certain ominous symptoms were beginning to shew themselves once more. The Bishop was found as usual writing, and as soon as the doctor left the room insisted on returning to his work, so intense was his desire to com-plete what he had in hand. It was the spirit of the Vener-able Bede once again. He passed away on the following Saturday afternoon (St Thomas's Day, 1889).

I should convey quite a wrong impression if I pictured Dr Lightfoot as a scholar mainly, shut up in his study and devoted to his patristic writings. Throughout he took the deepest interest in men and affairs and had a quick perception of the beauties of nature, whether expressed in flowers or in noble scenery.

His diocesan activities naturally found their centre in his Cathedral city where he met regularly on diocesan engagements his principal clergy and laity. But he went everywhere, and in the chief towns in his Diocese, especially—Darlington, Gateshead, South Shields, Stock-ton, Sunderland and the Hartlepools—his presence and powerful advocacy in the pulpit and on the platform were well known.

The article in the *Quarterly Review* referred to already enters so fully into that side of his life that I need not enlarge upon it. Nor need I mention the wonderful re-sponse made to his appeal in January 1884 for twenty-five new churches and mission halls. Five years later he was able to report that "no less than forty-five churches and mission chapels have been completed, or will shortly be so, through the instrumentality of the fund". The public meetings in support of this great cause, and the actual consecrations of the churches erected brought him con-stantly before his people at the happiest moments in a happy life.

The joys of his holidays he delighted to share with his Chaplains and three or four of the sons of the house. Braemar and Norway he specially loved; and those who were with him in Norway will recollect on one occasion the entirely absorbed and unconcerned way in which he sat in a cariole correcting proof-sheets while being driven down precipitous paths by a small boy.

The Bishop's generosity flowed out at all times and in many directions, from the Lightfoot Church Institute built at Bishop Auckland at the beginning of his ministry, to the noble Church of St Ignatius the Martyr,

Hendon, designed to be "a thankoffering for seven years of a happy episcopate", but actually consecrated by him on July 2nd of the last year of his life. To the ordinary channels for diocesan expenditure, deepened and broad-ened by his strong leadership, he gave a very generous and continuous support. But I think it gave him the greatest happiness to help forward individuals and especially young men such as the sons of the house, or the abler boys in the Castle choir. Reference to this is made elsewhere in this volume.

This generosity was the result of an abounding love, touched with emotion of no ordinary kind. It was a true comment made to a neighbour by one who saw him first when presiding at the Newcastle Congress: "Why, man, don't you see? He is all heart". Naturally shy and reserved, he would at times give an expression to his affection which was almost embarrassing. I can see him still as with the tears starting from his eyes he hurried across the great drawing-room at Auckland Castle to congratulate me upon my election to a Fellowship at King's College, Cambridge. Doubtless many others besides myself treasure precious letters—far too sacred for any other eye—in which affection and gratitude well forth with the tenderness of a true Father in God.

J. R. H. (1931)

Note—The Dean of Wells allows us to print a series of letters (in the Appendix, *Letters to a Chaplain*) which illustrate in a remarkable way what is said above by the Dean of Lichfield and Bishop Harmer.

Chapter XII

THE THEOLOGICAL INFLUENCE OF BISHOP LIGHTFOOT[1]

BY THE DEAN OF WELLS

IT is now forty-five years since I got Lightfoot's three Commentaries on St Paul's Epistles as my first College Prize. The earliest of these volumes had appeared thirteen years before, in 1865. He had taken his degree in 1851 as Senior Classic and thirtieth Wrangler, gaining also the first of the Chancellor's medals. He was elected a Fellow of Trinity in the next year: "When Mr Lightfoot makes one of his charges", said the Master, W. H. Thompson, "there is no resisting him". He lectured on classical authors and hoped to edit Aeschylus. When I was lecturing on the *Agamemnon*, thirty years later, I found nothing so helpful as the manuscript notes of his lectures. In 1861 he succeeded Bishop Ellicott as Hulsean Professor of Divinity. The Commentary on Galatians was his first book. Its Preface reveals the man. Let us hear him speak:

> The general plan and execution of the work will commend or condemn themselves: but a few words may be added on one or two points which require explanation.
>
> It is no longer necessary, I trust, to offer any apology for laying aside the received text. When so much conscientious labour has been expended on textual criticism, it would be unpardonable in an editor to acquiesce in readings which for the most part are recommended neither by intrinsic fitness nor by the sanction of antiquity.

[1] This paper was read at a meeting of the Auckland Brotherhood at Lambeth Palace on June 27th, 1923. The intimacy of the occasion will account for the freedom and familiarity of treatment.

This was a new and bold line in those days for a commentator to take. After naming the principal workers on textual criticism, and explaining why he could not adopt any existing text, but must needs construct one for himself, he continues:

> Moreover I was encouraged by the promise of assistance from my friends the Rev. B. F. Westcott and the Rev. F. J. A. Hort, who are engaged in a joint recension of the Greek Testament, and have revised the text of this Epistle for my use. Though I have ventured to differ from them in some passages and hold myself finally responsible in all, I am greatly indebted to them for their aid.

This was by no means the only innovation which the commentary presented. His independence of predecessors was startling. Wordsworth we knew; Alford we knew; Ellicott we knew; but nothing like this had appeared, if we omit for various reasons Stanley's *Corinthians* and Jowett's commentaries, which broke new ground indeed, but not with the same mastery of language and of history. Wordsworth gave us the Fathers in abundance; Alford and Ellicott the Germans. Of Alford, Gwatkin used to say that when he began to take pupils he bought a copy of Alford to see where all their mistakes came from. Ellicott's verbal accumulations were crushing or smothering: Lightfoot in the Preface says of him quite kindly that he "has subjected the Apostle's language to a minute and careful scrutiny".

Lightfoot's notes are terse and masculine: he is never tedious or ambiguous. He refuses to catalogue the interpretations of previous writers; he will not even mention the names of other commentators, unless there is some very special reason. Listen to his comments on Galatians iii. 20, "A mediator is not mediator of one, but God is one":

> The number of interpretations of this passage is said to mount up to

250 or 300. Many of these arise out of an error as to the mediator, many more disregard the context, and not a few are quite arbitrary. Without attempting to discuss others which are not open to any of these objections, I shall give that which appears to me the most probable.

One precious feature of this commentary which was also quite new is the plain summary prefixed to each paragraph of the Epistle. Here in vigorous English, such as the Apostle himself might have used had he been writing in our tongue, is a statement of the meaning of the Greek which the notes that follow are intended to justify. Put these summaries together and you may read the Epistle through in modern English. It is this lucidity which makes these commentaries differ from all others, even (may I say it?) from the commentaries on St John and the Epistle of the Hebrews which his distinguished colleague was producing at his side.

Another characteristic is the insistent recognition that the Greek of St Paul was not a debased language, loosely constructed and uncontrolled by the ordinary laws of grammar. Lightfoot's classical training in the severe Cambridge school, which produced Thompson and Jebb and Mayor and Monro, not to speak of Jackson and Verrall and Peile, prepared him to treat the Greek of the New Testament, and especially of St Paul, as a form of the language distinct indeed from that of the classical period, but no less certainly ruled by a grammar which would reveal itself to systematic study. His friend Moulton, the Head Master of the Leys school, was hard at work on a revised edition of Winer's *New Testament Grammar*. It is true that Moulton's brilliant son—lost, alas, in a steamer sunk in the war—lived long enough to produce the first part of a work which would have made his father stare. But the new material for the study of

Hellenistic Greek, which was supplied in bewildering abundance by the papyrus finds in Egypt, had revolutionised the conceptions of the period between 1865 and 1881—the only too memorable year when the Revised Version of the New Testament was published. Words and phrases which had seemed unique, or had been strained in the attempt to interpret them by the scanty parallels to be discovered in the literature previously extant, now fell into place, and the grammar by which they were ruled found abundant illustration. It is one of the tragedies of scholarship that the revision was made a generation too soon. But the principles on which Lightfoot and Westcott and Hort and Moulton had insisted were vindicated by discoveries which they could not have anticipated, and the later results would hardly have been achieved if they had not laid the foundation as faithfully as they did.[1]

The Commentary on Philippians followed in 1868. Lightfoot rejoiced in exchanging the dogmatic controversy of the Galatians for the serener atmosphere of the Roman Captivity.

We have passed at once (he says in the Preface) from the most dogmatic to the least dogmatic of the Apostle's letters, and the transition is instructive. If in the one the Gospel is presented in its opposition to an individual form of error, in the other it appears as it is in itself....If we would learn what he held to be its essence, we must ask ourselves what

[1] Lightfoot's prevision of this possibility is strikingly illustrated by words from a lecture delivered in 1863 (quoted by Professor Milligan in his *Selections from the Greek Papyri*, p. xx): "You are not to suppose that the word (some New Testament word which had its only classical authority in Herodotus) had fallen out of use in the interval, only that it had not been used in the books which remain to us: probably it had been part of the common speech all along. I will go further, and say that if we could only recover letters that ordinary people wrote to each other without any thought of being literary, we should have the greatest possible help for the understanding of the language of the New Testament generally".

is the significance of such phrases as "I desire you in the heart of Jesus Christ", "To me to live is Christ", "That I may know the power of Christ's resurrection", "I have all strength in Christ that giveth me power". Though the Gospel is capable of doctrinal exposition, though it is eminently fertile in moral results, yet its substance is neither a dogmatic system, nor an ethical code, but a Person and a Life.

There speaks the Lightfoot that we knew.

This second instalment of the series of commentaries on St Paul which he had planned at the outset, when he parcelled out the New Testament with his colleagues Hort and Westcott, offers the best illustration of another characteristic of his work as a commentator. He was essentially a historian, and he dreaded losing himself in textual criticism and linguistic interpretation. He wanted to see the man who wrote these letters and to portray the period in which he lived. "Above all", he once said to me, "write dissertations." Two dissertations were appended in this volume, one on "St Paul and Seneca", the other—famous and fruitful still after more than half a century—on "The Christian Ministry".

For all his acquaintance with the history of theology, Lightfoot was not a theologian. The mystical and philosophic qualifications essential to the true theologian were endowments granted in rich measure to his fellow-workers, the former to Westcott, the latter to Hort; but they were no part of Lightfoot's equipment for his task. All three had the love of truth in the smallest details and the training in scholarship which are indispensable to the interpreter of Scripture. All three were independent thinkers and intensely religious and devout. But each had his own bent, and Lightfoot's natural line was that of history. His article on "Eusebius", the father of ecclesiastical history, in the *Dictionary of Christian Biography*, is a treatise in itself, and the one contribution that he actually made to that history of the Church in the fourth century which at one time he had eagerly desired to write.

It so happened that the most serious attack on Chris, tianity which its defenders had to meet in the sixties was on its historical side. The Tübingen school, under the leadership of Ferdinand Christian Baur, had rewritten the early story of the Church on the hypothesis that St Paul was at daggers drawn with St Peter and the other leading Apostles, and that most of the books of the New Testament had been written to conceal this fundamental opposition between the Apostles of the Circumcision and the Apostle of the Gentiles. Only three of the Pauline Epistles were undoubtedly genuine and trust, worthy. Above all, the Acts of the Apostles was the most brilliant and successful of forgeries. It was "ten, denziöz"—to use their favourite epithet; written after the conflict was at an end with the definite design of covering up the last traces of it: the Catholic Church was founded on the Apostles and required that from the beginning there should have been complete harmony among its founders. Lightfoot was supremely qualified to be the champion of the Faith on such a field as this. His dissertation on "St Paul and the Three" in his first commentary, and three dissertations on "the Essenes" in relation to Christianity, contained in the volume on Colossians, were but fragments of the contribution which he ultimately made to the defence of the received account of the Christian origins. It was not until 1875 that this last volume appeared. I can well remember the glee with which in my copy of 1878 I underlined the words of the Preface: "I venture to hope that my previous commentaries have established my claim to be regarded as an independent worker". His position in-deed was secure: a second edition of the new commentary was called for within nine months of the first. But the series came to an abrupt close. He still gave his powerful lectures on other Epistles of St Paul in preparation for its continuance, and he also lectured on the Acts of the Apostles.

My own studies were not in divinity, and the one time I heard him was when in my third year of residence I ventured into the Hall of Trinity College and listened to his lecture on St Stephen's speech, just after he had re-ceived the call to Durham. His work on the New Testa-ment was at an end. Some of you will remember the illuminated address of welcome presented to him in Auckland Castle by a group of enthusiastic admirers, in which, in well-meant if not well-chosen words, they expressed the hope that "many more Epistles of St Paul might flow from his Lordship's pen". But it was not to be. A few fragments of commentary, gathered from lecture-notes, were piously edited for the Lightfoot Trustees by one of our brotherhood—only enough to deepen regret that the master's pen was for ever laid aside.

This slight account of Lightfoot's contribution to New Testament study would be sadly imperfect if we did not add that he learned enough of Coptic to write an im-portant chapter on the Sahidic and Bohairic MSS. for Scrivener's *Introduction to the Textual Criticism of the New Testament*. He also picked up a little Armenian, of which hardly another English scholar knew a word at that time; but this particular venture led to a somewhat humiliating disappointment. He had taken of necessity an interest in what could be discovered as to the lost *Diatessaron* of Tatian—the four Gospels arranged in a

Harmony—he had written about it in the brilliant articles in the *Contemporary Review*, in which he disposed once for all of the unknown author of "Supernatural Religion", who, under a veil of anonymity, had made a gross attack on the *bona fides* of Dr Westcott. While these articles were in progress there appeared at Venice in 1876—though the book was not known in England for several years later—Moesinger's Latin translation of the Commentary on Tatian by Ephraem the Syrian, which was preserved only in Armenian. In a note appended to the reprint of his articles in 1889, Lightfoot tells how he had had the original on his shelf all the time without being aware of it:

> I had for some years possessed a copy of this work in four volumes (namely, the Armenian translation of some of Ephraem's works, published in 1836), and the thought had more than once crossed my mind that possibly it might throw light on Ephraem's mode of dealing with the Gospels, as I knew that it contained notes on St Paul's Epistles or some portion of them. I did not then however possess sufficient knowledge of Armenian to sift its contents, but I hoped to investigate the matter when I had mastered enough of the language. Meanwhile...

Alas for that "Meanwhile": for it meant that the credit of an important discovery was by a tiresome mischance lost to our English scholarship. It is a small point, no doubt; but Lightfoot's record would be incomplete, if we did not remember how widely he had cast his net.

Side by side with his New Testament commentaries Lightfoot was engaged on what he intended to be a complete edition of the so-called Apostolic Fathers—the earliest extant writings outside the New Testament. The first instalment appeared in 1869, and consisted of all that was known of the Epistle of Clement of Rome, and of the misnamed Second Epistle, a homily of the latter part of the second century. These works were edited with the same attention to their textual criticism, the same carefulness of comment, and the same accompaniment of Introductions, as had distinguished his biblical commentaries.

Then the discovery of the missing parts of both works in a Greek manuscript (the manuscript from which was afterwards published the *Didache*), and also in a Syriac version, led him in 1877 to issue a supplementary volume to complete the first until a second edition of the whole could be undertaken.

On this second edition he was actually at work on his death-bed. The two substantial volumes were practically finished. The Preface was not written, and its place is taken by a Prefatory Note by the lifelong friend who had succeeded him at Durham. Here we learn how, under conditions of great weakness, "he retained his passion for work and was busy with Clement till he fell into a half-conscious state three days before his death. The last words which he wrote formed part of an imperfect sentence of the fragmentary essay on St Peter's visit to Rome".

We turn with a pathetic interest to these closing words. I shall quote to you almost half of the third and unfinished section. You will feel that his eye was not dimmed nor his intellectual force abated. There is no rough draft from which it might be supplemented: for his manner was to master his subject in all its details and plan out his dissertation in advance, and then write with a free pen, quoting his authorities from memory, so as not to impede the flow of his thought, and leaving the verification of his references till his writing was done. The essay is entitled "Saint Peter in Rome": its first section is headed "The Promise and its Fulfilment", the second "The Roman visit of Peter": these occupy twenty pages. Then comes the third, "The Twenty-five Years' Episcopate".

The twenty-five years of St Peter's episcopate had at one time a sentimental and might almost be said to have a dogmatic value. It was unique in the history of the papacy. Though the records of certain periods of its career, more especially its earliest career, are scanty, we know enough to say with certainty that no later bishops of Rome held the see for a quarter of a century until our own day. Now however all is changed. The papacy of Pio Nono has been unique in many ways. It has seen the declaration of papal infallibility: it has witnessed the extinction of the temporal power; and, last of all, it has exceeded by more than a year the reputed term of St Peter. The twenty-five years therefore have ceased to have any dogmatic or sentimental importance; and in dealing with them critically, we need have no fear lest we should be doing violence to any feelings which deserve respect. But there is still a prior question to be settled before we discuss the length of St Peter's episcopate. Was he Bishop of Rome at all?[1]

After pointing out that St Paul is not spoken of as Bishop of any of the churches that he founded, the essayist continues: "I cannot find that any writers for the first two centuries or more speak of St Peter as Bishop of Rome". Half a dozen more sentences and the fragment is at an end. Our loss is the less serious, since the conclusion is foregone, and the order of the first five Bishops had already been fully treated in what Hort speaks of as "the great essay on the Early Succession of the Roman Bishops".

Thus much for St Clement of Rome. Of St Ignatius I cannot do better than quote Hort's words from that article in the *Dictionary of National Biography*, the strain of writing which exhausted his failing vitality, but was a glad sacrifice to the friendship of a lifetime:

The edition of Ignatius and Polycarp, which forms the second part of Lightfoot's *Apostolic Fathers*, "was the motive", he tells us, "and the core of the whole". He was fascinated by the Ignatian problem nearly

[1] *Apostolic Fathers*, Part I, ii, 501.

thirty years before his first edition appeared (2 vols. in 3, 1885; 2nd edit., 3 vols., 1889). Originally, like many unprejudiced students, he accepted as genuine only those three (or rather abridgements of three) out of seven Ignatian epistles which Cureton had found in an early Syriac manuscript; and the notes which Lightfoot originally wrote were framed on this assumption. He never saw any probability in the opinion still held by many, that all the seven alike are spurious, and at last he convinced himself that the seven epistles unabridged were genuine. He was partly led to this result by the arguments of Zahn's *Ignatius von Antiochien* (1873). The masterly defence of the conclusions thus slowly reached has already [and that is now more than thirty years ago] produced a clear though hardly decisive effect on critical opinion, in spite of the strong prepossessions which it has had to encounter. After all, however, this discussion occupies only 120 out of nearly 2000 pages, and the whole book is of a quality that needs no adventitious flavour of controversy.

This judgment perhaps errs on the side of caution: Hort was too keenly interested not to dread exaggeration in estimating the chief critical achievement of his friend. I am not aware that Lightfoot's position is seriously challenged anywhere to-day, though I have ventured to question whether his acceptance of the record of St Polycarp's martyrdom can be regarded as final.

It was in these great volumes on the Apostolic Fathers that Lightfoot found free course as a historian. He had— if I may adopt a phrase which he himself employed in another context—knocked the last "nail in the coffin of the Tübingen theory". But he had done much more: his work was never merely negative. He had given vividness and security to the stories of the early Martyrs, and had unravelled the relation of the various Emperors to the growing Church. He had set a standard of minute carefulness, which left no stone unturned in the investigation of historical documents, and an example of independence which led Harnack to say of him that "he never defended a tradition for the tradition's sake". His clear

exposition made him eminently readable: in his Dissertations there is sometimes more than a touch of rhetoric
which he knew how to control. "History", says Hort
again, "meant not less to him as a man than as a scholar. He
found in it, he said, the best cordial for drooping spirits."

How shall we conclude? The Great Three dwarfed
their contemporaries and their immediate successors.
Their intimate co-operation among themselves was an
increase of power to each; but the very sufficiency (αὐτάρκεια) which it produced resulted in a kind of isolation.
As they did not feel the need, so they did not seek the
assistance of the younger generation of would-be workers
in the same fields. Their books and their lectures made an
immediate and abiding impression; personally they were
always eager to assist if asked, but they made no advances.
Hort was the least approachable of the three: he had a
nervous manner of speech which rather terrified the
modest enquirer. Moreover, he positively dreaded the
possibility that what he said might bias the judgment of a
younger man whom he believed to be starting in a right
spirit on an important investigation. No trouble was too
great for him to take in answer to a direct question on
some obscure point: it was fascinating to watch him go
the round of his books: but there was no offer either to
criticise or to supervise.

Lightfoot was quite different. Easy of approach, whole-
heartedly sympathetic, but almost dumb. "Well, what
do you think yourself?"—how well I remember it: and
then no more till we were half-way back again from the
top of the Park; and then, as if by a sudden inspiration,
in the intervals of heavy patting of his big dog ("Lion,
old boy! Come here, Lion: Good dog!"): "Go in for
Origen: he made so much"; and so on, till we got home.
But again, while there was eager encouragement and a

generous welcome of first efforts, there was no readiness to guide or control.

But at least these great ones cultivated in others the spirit of independence and exhaustive research. "I should advise you to take your New Testament, and form your own opinion first", was Hort's answer when I asked him to tell me which of the many Germans I ought to read in making a beginning in the Synoptic Problem. And Lightfoot, when Origen was in question, said: "Begin to write as soon as you possibly can. That was what Prince Lee always said to us. That is the way to learn. Almost all I have learnt has come from writing books. If you write a book on a subject, you have to read everything that has been written about it." Independence of judgment and the neglect of no detail—more valuable lessons in the end than any that a fostering guidance might have given.

"We grew up under Westcott and Hort", said a Cambridge Professor the other day: but he added with his quiet humour, "like plants under a cedar tree." I am not quite prepared to endorse the *mot*. They were taken from us in one way or another all too soon, and then we began to sprout each after his kind. We were oppressed, but not overwhelmed, by the sense of our ignorance. We felt that they had left a work which demanded to be carried on. If no one of us could venture to attempt it by himself, something might come of a joint effort. We were not lacking in independence of spirit, we had been taught to take pains. We began to write as soon as we could, and we learned by writing. But we never ceased to be conscious how inferior was the breed of the "Epigoni", inferior in intellectual vigour and in power of concentration, but inferior above all in that intensity of moral and religious conviction which makes the worker so much greater than his work.

Chapter XIII

BISHOP LIGHTFOOT'S PLACE AS A HISTORIAN

BY THE BISHOP OF GLOUCESTER

I have been asked to write a short estimate of Bishop Lightfoot's place as a historian, and I gladly comply with the request. Any value in the judgment which I express will arise very largely from the fact that I never came in any way under his personal influence. I only once met him, when I stayed for a night at Auckland Castle. Although my home was in Durham during all the years of his episcopate, and though I was present at his enthronement in Durham Cathedral, and also at his funeral, I was resident during all that time in Oxford, and never came in contact with him personally. Through all those years I never heard him preach, and only once make a speech. Although I heard about his administration of the Diocese, and had learnt in every way to respect him, I was never influenced in any way by him personally.

My judgment is based purely on his writings. When I was at school I read his Commentaries on St Paul's Epistles, but the important event for me was that his edition of *Ignatius* was published just after I had taken my degree, when I was beginning the formal study of theology and obtained a Fellowship, which enabled me to devote myself with leisure and freedom to that study. For myself, as for Church history, the publication of Lightfoot's *Ignatius* represented a quite definite epoch. It was the definite assertion of the scientific method of study over the speculative for early Church history. May I make extracts from what I wrote some years ago?

In an article on "Methods of Early Church History", delivered first as Birkbeck Lecturer at Trinity College, Cambridge, I wrote:

> The strife of contending opinions has made the need of scientific investigation more and more apparent, and three different schools in England, France, and Germany have developed in a distinguished degree historical methods. One is Anglican, a second Romanist, a third Protestant or rationalist in its origin. With one is associated the name of Lightfoot, with the second that of Duchesne, with the third that of Harnack. It is not necessary to dwell in this country on the work of Lightfoot or of those associated with him. There may be some who are attracted more by the subtlety and versatility of Hort; but there is a greatness in the profound simplicity of Lightfoot to which Hort does not rise. We must judge men by their productions; and the edition of the New Testament is not the equal of what Harnack calls the greatest patristic monograph of the century—a monograph which has been the most important factor in changing the current of critical opinion.[1]

And, again, in a review of Lightfoot's *Apostolic Fathers*, published first in the *Quarterly Review*, I wrote:

> There are solid attainable facts even in early Church history, and that there are such is due above all to the labours of a great English scholar. Bishop Lightfoot was one of the greatest, if not the greatest, of modern English bishops, but he was more than that; he was not only the munificent administrator of a populous northern diocese, adapting the Church of the past to the needs and aspirations of the present, but he also occupied a foremost position among the investigators of Christian Antiquity. It is the purpose of this essay, making use of the definite results that Dr Lightfoot arrived at, results which the lapse of time since his death has only served to establish more surely, to construct so far as we are able a picture of Christianity at its most obscure and crucial epoch, the beginning of the second century. We believe that in doing so we shall be performing a by no means useless task, for Bishop

[1] *History, Authority and Theology*, pp. 253–254.

Lightfoot's works, although he writes throughout in a singularly clear and attractive style, and marshals an intricate subject with great skill, deal of necessity so largely in the technicalities of scholarship as to confuse an untrained reader.[1]

And again:

Baur succeeded so far as the question he asked was right; he failed because his method was wrong. His object was historical; his method was not scientific. He approached the subject with *a priori* ideas, derived from the philosophy of Hegel. He developed a theory based on a one-sided study of a small number of documents, and then proceeded to rearrange the dates of the remainder in a manner which would suit his preconceived notions. The opposition to Baur has created a scientific method. The futility of opposing orthodoxy to orthodoxy, the old Christian dogmas to the new Tübingen dogmas, became clear. A method which would enable the date of documents to be fixed, on evidence which would appeal to the unbiassed investigator, was necessary. Such a method has been founded, and is being developed at the present day; and we do not think that we can be accused of insular prejudice in claiming a foremost place in that work for the English, or, more accurately, for the Cambridge school of Church history—for, although it has spread elsewhere, Cambridge is its home. The most scientific works that have been published on Church history are Lightfoot's editions of the Apostolic Fathers.[2]

I can remember now the pleasure with which I studied Lightfoot's *Ignatius* when it first appeared. The attractiveness of its method, of its sobriety of judgment, of its comprehensiveness. One felt quite clearly that here we were on solid ground. The distinguishing features of the work were, first of all, its scholarly accuracy. No pains were spared in fixing accurately the texts of the works to be studied and in a careful exegesis. In many cases the conclusions arrived at were made possible because there was a correct text of the documents, because glosses had been eliminated, and incorrect interpretations corrected. The next point which appealed to me was the scientific

---

[1] *History, Authority and Theology*, p. 279.   [2] *Ibid.* p. 282.

method. The whole of the external evidence was carefully collected on every historical point which had to be discussed, and the breadth of the evidence collected re-moved the discussion of internal testimony from the pre-cariousness which so often distinguishes it. Then next, one was impressed by the completeness of the work. Nothing which might throw light on it was omitted. There are few really who have not only the learning and industry but what I may call the intellectual massiveness which enables them to grasp every side of a problem. Again and again one notices how precarious are the results which have been attained by guesses, often brilliant, based upon a portion of the evidence. Lightfoot had the power, the industry, and the thoroughness to neglect no side of the evidence before him. Then, lastly, there was the sobriety of judgment. That is the trained historical sense which comes from the continued exercise of the critical faculty. We feel that the result is right and true; we feel that the writer has not allowed himself to be carried away by the attractiveness of a specious theory.

The result of Lightfoot's work has been that since then the study of Church history has gone on on different lines from those which formerly prevailed. Certain questions are definitely settled. The old uncertainty about the dates of books is reduced within definite limits. I think on almost every main point which Lightfoot discussed, his judgment has prevailed. The one exception is the Johannine literature, and there our judgment must still be uncertain. The world of scholars is not prepared to accept the genuineness of the Fourth Gospel in the way that it accepts the genuineness of the Ignatian Epistles, but what will be the final verdict, I don't think any of us is quite prepared to say.

But Lightfoot had other and even greater qualities as a historian. He was an accurate scholar, he was a scientific investigator, but he was much more. The pages of *The Apostolic Fathers* are illuminated by the living interest, by the historical imagination, by the spiritual insight which is necessary for a great historian; and in Lightfoot's work on *Leaders in the Northern Church*, those gifts of historical imagination and insight are conspicuous.

Bishop Lightfoot had always contemplated a great work on *The History of Christian Literature*. We can deplore the loss of it, although the ten years of his administration of the Diocese of Durham is an adequate compensation. For, after all, when the example has been set, other men can carry on the work. The pages of *The Apostolic Fathers* are a mine of information and judgment on many of the most disputed questions of early Church history. His encyclopaedic article on Eusebius should be the prolegomena of the edition of that author, which should some day be produced. There are still many problems which demand a thorough and careful investigation, but the attention of living theologians is attracted rather in other directions. The real fact is that the scientific criticism which began with Lightfoot has attained almost as great an amount of certainty as is possible about the historical facts of early Christianity. We know that the great body of the Pauline Epistles are genuine, if not the Pastorals; we have advanced nearly as far as is possible in the solution of the Synoptic problem; we have no doubt that the Acts of the Apostles and St Luke's Gospel were by the author that tradition assigns to them. We have not solved the Johannine problem, but we know that the writings ascribed to St John cannot be much later at the latest than the beginning of the second century. We know the dates of the Apostolic Fathers. So though there are many interesting historical problems still awaiting solution, the attention of Christian writers had turned away to more intricate problems of theology and philosophy. The possibility of that is mainly due to the influence of Lightfoot and the historical school with which his name will always be associated.

In conclusion perhaps I may bear witness to the profound simplicity of character, deep personal piety, the broad-minded sympathy, the sane theological judgment which inspires all his writings. As a preacher he always wrote his sermons. They were always massive and scholarly. They might seem to be above the heads of a simple congregation, but his great personality was always behind the writings, and there is abundant evidence how, in many a remote village of his diocese, his visit, and the sermon that he preached, and his inspiring personality were remembered for a whole generation.

Chapter XIV

THE LIGHTFOOT SCHOLARSHIPS FOR ECCLESIASTICAL HISTORY

BY THE REV. J. P. WHITNEY, D.D.

Dixie Professor of Ecclesiastical History, Cambridge

THE generous foundation of the Lightfoot Scholarships by Dr Lightfoot, then Hulsean Professor, dates from 1870, and the first of them was awarded in 1874. They were founded, it is said, in gratitude for Dr Westcott's return to Cambridge. Their usefulness and their influence, direct and indirect, ever since then have fulfilled the founder's wishes and proved his wisdom. He himself always looked at Christianity and studied it first and last from the historical standpoint, and with absolute historical accuracy. The idea of this foundation was also that of the joint comprehensive work on Christian origins which the three great Cambridge Professors planned at the time of *Essays and Reviews*, his share of which Dr Lightfoot most nearly completed. To much the same impulse we may ascribe the foundation in 1884 of the Dixie Professorship of Ecclesiastical History by Emmanuel College after Dr Hort had come to it as Fellow. And we may even go further back to another great Cambridge scholar, Hugh James Rose, who hoped and worked for a revival of English Church life, based on historical study.

For many years the list of books drawn up by the founder was in force, and it made an admirable, solid foundation for continuous knowledge likely to inspire and suggest lines of further study. I know both from what others have told me, and from my own experience, the excellent wise guidance it gave. The books thus set were:

DE BROGLIE: *L'Église et l'Empire Romaine.*
BRYCE: *Holy Roman Empire.*
GUIZOT: *Histoire de la Civilisation en France.*
MILMAN: *History of Latin Christianity.*
RANKE: *History of the Popes.*
   History of the Reformation.

In the regulations, which are taken from the Founder's Deed, the special object of the foundation is defined as "the encouragement of the study of Ecclesiastical History in itself, and in connection with General History", and the range and choice in both cases was limited to the period between the accession of Marcus Aurelius in A.D. 161 and the Fall of the Roman Empire in 1806.

Of these books, De Broglie is the only one out of date; Guizot is still most useful, so is Milman for his sweep and use of original authorities; the three others are classics. And it will be noticed that a large general knowledge is required.

By an excellent provision the two examiners each year were to be one an Oxford and one a Cambridge man, and we must acknowledge gratefully the continual and brotherly interest of our colleagues from Oxford. They, like the Cambridge examiners, have given most useful help, and have, again like them, often kept up an interest in the scholars they examined. Many of these have had the same good fortune as myself; I was examined by Dean Kitchin and that really remarkable Cambridge man Archdeacon Cheetham, both of whom were always in later years very kind to me and took an interest in my work.

Speaking of the mere examinations, it must be noted what results have come from the yearly prescription of Special Subjects by the original scheme. It was his special subject, John of Salisbury, that turned the late Dr Figgis to the study of Political Thought, and much the same thing has happened in other cases. In this, as in other ways, the foundation worked in the direction of the founder's own studies. His example had been powerful in moulding Cambridge men in the past and may, I think, do so even more in the future.

Looking down the list of scholars since 1874, it will be seen that many of them have written much and are well-known historians. Some of them have also done first-rate work in the teaching of our Cambridge School. That School would indeed be poor if these names did not belong to it, and if some of them have since turned to other branches of study rather than the ecclesiastical, they have all been better historians for their early work, and so they have carried what I may call the Lightfoot impulse into wider fields. Some of them have told me what they owe to that early influence.

I do not speak of later years, but some of even the very late scholars have already given us first-rate work and are teaching excellently. An Oxford examiner once told me, when I was his colleague, how he envied Cambridge the existence of such an incentive to study Church history; that year there were five candidates, all of whom we thought very creditable young Church historians. We cannot limit the influence of the Foundation merely to the winners of the Scholarships. These short notes indicate what the founder of the Scholarships did for Cambridge. His gift showed both what he was in himself, and what he wished his learners to be.

Many years of study have made me feel more and more his pre-eminence as a historian of the early Church. His knowledge, patristic as well as historical, was vast, and no one can turn, again and again, as I have done, to his studies of St Clement, St Ignatius and St Polycarp, without learning something fresh every time, even for other than the early period (I am thinking especially of his pages on the Church of San Clemente at Rome, and on the learning of Grosseteste). Comparing him with other historians of the same rank, he had the rare merit of presenting the evidence apart from his own conclusions and opinions, so that any reader could form his own views independently: hence no one is a better guide for a student. He lived, as it were, with the characters about whom he wrote in their age, and he had learnt for himself the great lesson of continuity throughout Church history from the fundamental revelation of Christ downwards. So he is the best of teachers as well as a great historian, for he sought to train other individuals as he had trained him-self. It was wonderful how his great Northern See appealed to him by its history. To the great actors in it he did full and yet delicately sympathetic justice. He lived in its history as he had done in earlier times, and taught us to know and love the Apostles of the North. Fresh responsibilities and a great historic place gave him even a broader view and a deeper grasp of continuity and Christian life on the historical side, much as in other ways they did for his great colleague and successor. Some later writers may lack his balance and exaggerate, but his own achievement remains.

This coherence and solidity of view is found in his sermons too. I remember as a Freshman (1877) listening to an Advent Course of Sermons which he gave at

St Bene't's, Cambridge. I went to them with a scientific friend from Manchester, who was not then deeply reli/gious, but is now a keen philanthropist. They dealt with the place of those who would hardly call themselves Christians, and with the influence of Christianity upon them.

I shall never forget the impression made on me then. We were so deeply impressed that we realised what we missed by his leaving Cambridge. Long afterwards, when I read and re/read all his sermons, I saw that his vast knowledge, his really poetic vision, and the ex/quisite balance of everything, along with his expressive and sympathetic style, made him one of our greatest English preachers.

EPILOGUE

His life from childhood seems to have been strictly of one piece, pervaded by one continuous thread of earnest duty, plain uprightness and scrupulous fidelity. The very idea that Lightfoot in any circumstance at school or college could have been untrue to his own high standard of resolve and aim is to me inconceivable.... All of us who were brought into contact with him were swayed by the influence of his unobtrusive goodness, his patient diligence, his meek sanctity, and gentleness of strength.

A School friend, quoted in Cambridge Review.
January 23, 1890.

Chapter XV

A SERMON, PREACHED BEFORE THE
UNIVERSITY OF CAMBRIDGE

BY THE RIGHT REV. G. R. EDEN, D.D.

formerly Bishop of Wakefield, Honorary Fellow of Pembroke College

IN GREAT ST MARY'S CHURCH ON SUNDAY,
24 NOVEMBER 1929

PHIL. III. 13. *One thing I do.*

IT is almost a truism to say that the man who succeeds
in any noble achievement is one who sees the end
from the beginning, and pursues it throughout with
unswerving purpose. To him, among many lesser motives, there is always one which absorbs into itself all the
rest, and gives a disciplined unity to every thought and
action. Like the tiny red thread, which runs through
every inch of rope made in one of our English dockyards,
and stamps it as belonging to one of the services of the
King, so every strand of such a life is gathered round one
paramount motive, which, though hidden at the heart of
it, controls them all.

In one single word, which we translate by "one thing",
St Paul here lays bare to us the central motive and main-
spring of his converted life. It occurs in one of those
passionate outbursts of fervent devotion to Our Lord,
which so often break the argument he is putting forward.
Devotion to a Redeemer and Master—that is the "one
thing" that he pursues—"that I may know Him, that I
may win Christ". "I press on, I press on", he cries
twice over. "I forget the past landmarks of the course, as

I press on towards the mark for the prize—the prize of the high calling of God in Christ Jesus."

It is not my intention to expound this passage to-day, but to use it for another purpose, and in doing so to depart somewhat from the usual content of a University Sermon. I wish to recall some memories of a man of this single-minded duty-loving devotion, a distinguished Cambridge Scholar and Divine, Bishop Lightfoot of Durham. I have no special qualifications to attempt such a theme, beyond the fact that I was one of his pupils here, and during the whole of his Episcopate knew him more intimately probably than any other man now living. There is no biography of Lightfoot—at his own earnest desire—and all that can be done is to gather up some of the fragments that remain, as a tribute, however inadequate, which is at least humble and sincere.

His life naturally falls into two periods—the first at Cambridge, and the second at Durham—the first as a teacher and theologian, and the second as Bishop.

I. CAMBRIDGE

We can trace some of the early impulses in Lightfoot's character to a great schoolmaster, Prince Lee, afterwards first Bishop of Manchester, who (not unlike James Tate of Richmond School, Yorkshire) sent up from King Edward's School, Birmingham to his own college of Trinity many first class men. Within nine years, we are told, thirteen of Prince Lee's boys took first class honours, of whom five were Senior Classics, and eight Fellows of the College; while of the thirteen no less than twelve—including Bishops Westcott and Lightfoot and Archbishop Benson—took Holy Orders. Even at school he was noted for two qualities which ran, like the red thread in the rope, through his whole career, an immense capacity for hard work, and a reverent spirit of devotion.

At Cambridge, he read with Westcott, in whose hands neither the severity of Cambridge classical training, nor the consecration of all study to the Lord of all truth, were likely to suffer. After his brilliant degree he took pupils, and wrote many articles on classical and sacred subjects of such a character, that it was soon recognised that a star of unusual magnitude had risen on the horizon. He became very early first Hulsean and then Lady Margaret Professor of Divinity. But it is not his public career of which I would speak. If we could have looked beneath these distinctions, we should have seen a life of fixed determination and resolute self-discipline. Take for instance his normal day. It began with early Chapel, followed by a short walk before breakfast. The morning was occupied by lecturing, teaching and studying; but this usually went on, without a break, up to his early dinner in hall at half past four. Then a slight pause for recreation and seeing friends—though he never spent much time in social intercourse. And then about six o'clock his door was shut for study that went on often into the early morning hours! It seems almost superhuman. But his capacity for work was matched by a robust constitution—a constitution which once took him to the top of the Jungfrau and back in a single walk from the Rhône valley, accompanied, before the days of guides, by a shoemaker of the village of Fiesch. You see the "red thread" of dogged perseverance here. Yet who knows but that these Herculean labours may not have strained even that strong heart, which finally faltered and failed at the early age of only sixty-one?

LECTURES

His lectures are a vivid memory to those who attended them. Crowds thronged to hear him expound the Scriptures as surely they had not been expounded before. A Master of Trinity, not given to enthusiasm, described the Senate House passage as "black with the fluttering gowns" of students bent on hearing the young Professor. No lecture-room was eventually found sufficient, and the great Dining Hall of Trinity might be seen filled round its long tables by an audience which included not a few Fellows of Colleges.

COMMENTARIES

These lectures grew into his unrivalled Commentaries on St Paul's Epistles, which, with his unique works on the second-century Fathers, form a great part of his priceless literary gift to his beloved Church. His first Commentary (on the Galatians), published early in 1865, was a landmark in New Testament exposition. It broke fresh ground: largely in its form, which set a pattern for future Commentaries, and wholly in its lucidity, directness and moral and devotional application. It was recognised as a new thing. Two others followed on Philippians, and Colossians with Philemon.

And here I may pause to call attention to what seem to me to be the two striking features of all Lightfoot's literary work: its historical character and its central aim. Lightfoot's mind was essentially that of the historian. He has marked his sense of the value of the study of history by the founding of the Lightfoot Scholarship. There is little of the mystic about him, still less of the speculative philosopher. The problems of theology are approached along historical lines and decided largely on historical grounds. We must remember that when he first wrote history was a young science. The popular teaching of history was largely a matter of dry facts and dates. Now with the help of archaeology it has made past ages live again for us in fresh and picturesque scenes. Lightfoot was a pioneer in this kind of thorough historical research. His immense labour (though hidden under the surface) has lighted up the conditions of the early Church. The actors on the stage are living and breathing men and women. Take for instance the relations between St Paul and the other Apostles. Even chief Apostles are human. They have sharp differences. But while others have invented extravagant theories out of these oppositions, Lightfoot shows the essential unity of the first Church throughout. And incidentally he cheers and encourages us in our modern differences, as Ulysses cheered his mariners, "O passi graviora", by showing that they are no new thing and need not lead to disruption. "History", he says, "is an excellent cordial for the drooping courage."

And the second characteristic feature of all his lectures, sermons and books is nothing less than that "one thing" again, which inspired and controlled all his thought. His mind always turned, as the needle of the compass turns to the pole, to the central truths of Christianity. Whether he were dealing with large questions of sacred history and theology, or expounding some passage of Scripture, each point great or small, had its setting in the revelation of God in Jesus Christ. His treatment of the Church, as the body of Christ, or even of the Christian Sacraments, made them living things indeed in that One Person. There is no room for controversy on details of faith and practice. His words seem to be filled with human and divine light.

They lift us to lofty heights and spacious views, and a larger air for breathing. They appeal to the heart and conscience as well as to the mind. They satisfy the mind, and they win the heart. No wonder that his three volumes of St Paul's Epistles had an almost phenomenal sale. I know of no single commentator of whom it could be said that thousands of Christian pulpits must have lighted their torch at his flame. And I hope and pray that they do so still.

For we are confessedly, and especially since the war, in a state of, I will not say confusion but unsettlement in Church teaching and discipline. We need to come back in thought to the great central truths of God as revealed in Christ. There is too much pre-occupation with smaller and secondary things. In the call which our two Arch-bishops have made to us for more sacred study among clergy and people, I believe our great Cambridge theo-logians of Lightfoot's day have the message best calculated to draw us together again. For it is all centred round the Person of our Lord. And the nearer we draw to Him, the closer we shall draw together, as men who pull on one rope must fall into line.

HIS APOSTOLIC FATHERS

We must pass quickly to his other priceless contribution to sacred learning, his edition of *The Apostolic Fathers of the Second Century.* He himself counted his work on Ignatius of Antioch the most important of all he had done. It is difficult to understand this estimate, unless we recall the highly charged atmosphere of the theological thought of that day. There had suddenly developed one of the most serious attacks on the New Testament, from the historical side, led by some distinguished German theologians, and apparently supported by vast research and learning. If their theories were correct, it was not too much to say that many of the New Testament writings would have proved to be pious forgeries of the second century. Our faith would have been in vain. It seemed to us humbler students to be a battle of the giants for the citadel of the Faith. Unbelievers were ready with the taunt flung at the Psalmist, "If the foundations be destroyed, what can the righteous do?" (Ps. xi. 3). It was then that our English theologians, and especially that distinguished band of Cambridge theologians of Lightfoot's day—and may we not say more particularly Lightfoot himself?—seemed to be raised up specially to vindicate the truth of the Gospel. The issue turned upon the trustworthiness of the second-century Fathers. Lightfoot's monumental work was one of the deciding factors in the fight. A learned Professor at Moscow remarked in 1912, "It was your English scholars—Lightfoot, Westcott, Hort, Sanday and Armitage Robinson—who turned back and defeated the greatest modern threat to the truth of the Christian religion". A strange incident made Lightfoot an active protagonist in the fray. An anonymous English writer had published an apparently learned book on the negative side, entitled *Supernatural Religion*, which had a sudden vogue in this country. It had, however, incidentally charged Lightfoot's greatest friend, Dr Westcott, with intentional deceit. Stung by this accusation[1] against his friend Lightfoot wrote surely

[1] Although this is the motive implied in Bishop Lightfoot's own preface to the articles published some fifteen years later in book form, he tells us in the first article that the incentive to his writing them was, partly at least, his indignation at a cruel rumour which attributed them to a "learned and venerable prelate". This was actually Bishop Thirlwall, who had recently retired from the See of St David's. See Thirlwall's "Letters" by Perowne and Stokes, London, 1881, p. 379.

the most remarkable series of articles ever printed in the *Contemporary Review*—afterwards published in a volume of essays just before his death at the urgent request of his friends. The articles were never finished. There was no need; for under Lightfoot's searching criticism the foundation of the book had been destroyed.

Though the fires of argument have long since died down, those essays are well worth careful study as a rich storehouse of facts. And incidentally they reveal those qualities in Lightfoot which have met us before—his patient investigation of facts, his scrupulous fairness, his generosity to an opponent; above all, his absorbing motive of loyalty to Christ. Still more it is a lesson to us all how to conduct such a controversy—not by violent counterassertions, not by mere denunciation, which, as he says, "may be unjust and is certainly unavailing", not by endeavouring to "close the door of enquiry by the hand of authority", but by patient statement of facts, by reverence as well as reason, and above all, in a spirit of earnest devotion to Christ. His opponent had remarked on his "earnestness". "I am indeed in earnest", he replies, "as I believe him to be. But it seems to me that the motives for earnestness are more intense in my case than in his; for (to say nothing else) as I read history, the morality of the coming generations of Englishmen is very largely dependent on the answers which they give to the questions at issue between us." "I cannot pretend", he says again just fourteen years afterwards, "to be indifferent about the veracity of the records which profess to reveal Him, whom I believe to be not only the very Truth, but the very Life."

II. DURHAM

From Cambridge we follow him to a totally different sphere. After more than one offer of high preferment had been declined, there came early in 1879 the momentous call to the See of Durham—the first that had come to a man in Priest's Orders for more than two hundred years. Few men can have passed through such an agony of choice as we know he suffered. Friends were divided. Some thought it would be a loss to the Church if his literary work should be exchanged for an administrative office. Others, more far-seeing as it proved, and recognising his already great practical ability, urged him, against all his inclinations, to accept. The task itself at that moment would have appalled a weaker man. The county of Durham had just passed through a rapid expansion in industry. New teeming populations were on the ground, with scanty provision for their spiritual needs. New parishes, new churches, mission rooms and schools were urgently needed on a large scale. There was no adequate diocesan organisation, such as we know to-day. And the wave of prosperity in business, strong and sudden as it had been, was receding as quickly as it had come. Yet the choice was made—upon his knees, "wrestling with the Angel in prayer". And once made it was never regretted. With his characteristic singleness of aim he threw himself wholly into the new and strange work.

His welcome in the North was astonishing. And new life came with him to the ancient "Bishoprick" of the North. Those of us who had known it for many years could hardly believe our eyes. The visible change which came over it in those short ten years was almost incredible.

A new Diocese of Newcastle, new parishes and buildings and endowments—an entirely new diocesan organisation —these were the material signs of his energy. But there was something else much more significant. "In that long wakeful night", he tells us, "when the decision was finally made", there arose in his mind a fresh vision. He loved young men: he believed in them. He would people his stately palace with young men—a succession of University men seeking Holy Orders. They should be not his pupils only but his sons. The remarkable Auckland Brotherhood, carried on, on slightly different lines, by his two successors, Westcott and Moule, ultimately reached a total of 216 men, many of them with high degrees, and gave an incalculable fresh impulse to the ranks of the Ministry in the Diocese. Its distinctive notes were its freedom from party-lines, its character as a company of "Sons of the House", and that strange indefinite influence of a unique personality, of a real Father in God. In Lightfoot's time it was possible to have them literally as sons and guests in the house. He refused all payment for himself. The beautiful Chapel was our spiritual home. Nothing quite like it had been seen before: and it is not likely that the combination of circumstances which made it possible will quickly happen again. Bishop Westcott counts his creation of the Brotherhood as the greatest work of his life—"greater than his masterpieces of interpretation and criticism, greater than his masterpieces of masculine and yet passionate eloquence". But remarkable as it was, yet the influence which held it together was more remarkable still. Lightfoot among his "sons" is not easy to describe.

He never ceased to wonder at their devotion to him. Nor could we quite explain it ourselves. He had no

conspicuous social gifts, no brilliant conversation, no
commanding and handsome presence. But he had
strength and reality. It was a kind of spell, seen and felt,
but, like a mother's love, not to be analysed. He was
constantly with us. He radiated goodwill and affection,
but without words. When friendship is strong and intimate, a very small sign is enough to convey whole
worlds of love. After some personal interview he would
take both your hands, and even lay his head for a moment
on your shoulder, while his eyes filled with restrained
tears. But that was all—there were no more words. It
was a dumb magnetic influence. But you left that room
with a strange attraction—not to him only, but to One
in whose presence you felt he always moved.

Such was Lightfoot to his "sons".

His was a strong, manly, sensible religion. He had
little love of symbolism or elaborate forms in worship;
but like his great namesake Butler had a reverent care for
externals. In his last illness not a Sunday passed, even in
extreme exhaustion, without his receiving Holy Communion. Yet speaking of other acts of worship he used
these remarkable words, over which I have often pon-
dered: "Things that edify others do not edify me. I feed
upon four or five great ideas."

To the very last he was the same. Work was the breath
of his life. Within three days of his death he was working
amid intervals of exhaustion on his edition of *Clement of
Rome*. And at last the pen literally dropped from his
hand in an unfinished sentence—almost recalling the
death of another Durham saint and historian—the
Venerable Bede.

We need no closing exhortation. His life and writings
are his memorial. I have only given a scanty and in-

adequate account of a great scholar and saint, who was so human and yet altogether unlike other men. But I wanted, towards the close of an already long life, to lay one more wreath on the altar of his memory, as one who owes him an untold debt and bore him a deep affection. It may encourage some of those beginning their course of study to hear of one who from first to last devoted all his powers and all his time to his beloved Master, who learned here a stern self-discipline in his earliest years, who kept before him this "one thing"—one single paramount aim—to press toward the mark for the prize of the high calling of God in Christ Jesus.

Appendix A

LETTERS TO A CHAPLAIN

THE following extracts from letters illustrate what has been said in the Chapter on "The Scholar still at work".

They are from the Bishop to his Chaplain, Rev. J. Armitage Robinson (now Dean of Wells), either from Lollards' Tower or Auckland Castle.

They reveal Dr Lightfoot's extraordinary range of learning, and his infinite pains to verify references no less than his loyalty to his Chaplain, and devotion to his Auckland "sons".

They have a peculiar interest as giving indications of the final stages of the completion of the (Introductory) Vol. I of his *St Ignatius and St Polycarp* in 1884 and 1885, while the letter of July 1887 discloses the early demand for a new edition.

Thus the letter of May 19th, 1884, shews that his revision had reached "The Church and the Empire" section. For in that section (pp. 477–85, Ed. 1) he dealt at considerable length with the epitaph of Abercius, in the light of the discovery of a fragment of it by Mr (now Sir William) Ramsay at Hieropolis near Synnada in 1883. The new matter of these pages could not have been written, in their final form, before 1884, and it was for them that the Bishop required the journals which he asked to be sent to him.

Later in the year he gave an interesting résumé of the conclusions to be drawn from the Epitaph, in a paper which he read at the Carlisle Church Congress on October 1st, 1884.

The books which he desired to consult in February 1885 indicate that he was then engaged on the last section: "The Date of the Martyr-dom" (of St Polycarp) as appears from the use made of them on pp. 661–95.

So the Bishop is able on February 24th to write: "I am at length getting towards the very end of Ignatius and Polycarp". He finished it by the end of June, dating his Preface "S. Peter's Day 1885".

Lollards Tower,
Lambeth Palace.
May 19, 1884.

Would you send me

(*a*) Pitra's *Analecta Solesmensia*, Vol. II (I think it is Vol. II but possibly Vol. III) containing Saint Abercius. A large octavo vol. in paper back on the first shelf left hand above the ledge as you enter the anteroom to my study from the passage.

(*b*) Two numbers of the *Journal of Hellenic Studies*—I think the last two—containing respectively

  (i) The Tale of Saint Abercius by Ramsay.

  (ii) A paper of Ramsay's on the Sites of the cities of Asia Minor.

(*c*) *Durham Diocesan History* (Low), lying I think on the table in my study.

Feb. 11, 1885.

Would you have the goodness at your leisure to verify for me this quotation (which I find in Ussher, *Works*, VII, p. 356) Oribasius, *Lib. 9. Collect. Medicin. cap. 8.*

Μηνὸς Λώου φθίνοντος πέμπτῃ δ' ἂν ἀνατέλλοντος ἡλίου ὁ Κύων ἐπιτέλλειν παρ' ἡμῖν ἐν Περγάμῳ πεπίστευται.[1]

I do not understand the δ' ἄν. I do not know whether there is any standard edition.

All well here. A grand football match between the Church Institute and the Castle students to come off this afternoon; the event of the Season. There would doubtless be all sorts of remembrances if they knew I was writing.

Feb. 24, 1885.

"One good turn deserves another."

You sent such a satisfactory answer to my last question that I venture to trouble you again.

(1) Would you have the goodness to look out and send me from the University Library the books of which I enclose a list.

If you will leave them at Macmillans with directions, they will see that they are forwarded to me.

---

[1] "Our tradition at Pergamon is that the Dogstar rises on the 26th day of the month Lous at sunrise." [In the text as quoted *Apostolic Fathers*, i. 674 ἄν is omitted.]

I believe my numbers are correct, but please verify—and see whether; Hermes xv, p. 363 contains an article of Droysen's relating to an Ephesian Inscription; Rhein. Mus. xvii, p. 355, one of Ahrens on names of months (or some allied subject); Rhein. Mus. xxviii, p. 403, something about a Leyden MS. containing a *Hemerologium*.

(2) I want particularly articles of Unger in Fleckeisen's *Neue Jahrbücher*, 1884, pp. 545 sqq. 745 sqq. on (I think, the day called Σεβαστή).

These I suppose I cannot get from the University Library, but I am tolerably sure Prof. Mayor will be able to lend them to me. He shall have them back in two or three weeks. They may be put into Macmillans hands, and come in the same parcel.

(3) Would you at your leisure copy out for me from Waddington and Lebas *Inscriptions*, Asie Mineure, iii, 1611 (something about 19th Xanthicos) in 1676 (from Trajanopolis 6th Daisios styled Σεβαστή). If you do not know your way about the book, I am sure Mr Bradshaw will show you.

If Waddington says anything in his notes on either of these inscriptions which throws light on the Calendar please let me have it.

I am really at length getting towards the very end of Ignatius and Polycarp. I am sorry to give you all this trouble, and yet I am sure you will do it cheerfully if you can.

Ap. 30, 1887.

I am glad to learn from your letter that you had such a successful tour, and returned home safely.[1]

And now my object is to get at Dr Spyridion Lambros, and likewise if possible, to get someone to look at and (if necessary) collate the Athos MSS relating to Ignatius and Polycarp.

[1] The Dean of Wells writes: "In the Easter Vacation of 1887 I had visited Patmos to collate a MS of Origen's Philocalia. In Athens I met Professor Spyridion Lambros, who was well known for his work in cataloguing the Greek MSS at Mount Athos, and afterwards gained a brief notoriety as Prime Minister of Greece. On my return to Cambridge I translated an essay of his written in German, which contained a collation of portions of the Shepherd of Hermas from an Athos codex. The edition of this, with a preface and two appendices, early in 1888, was my first literary effort. It is the book referred to in a subsequent letter (May 1, 1888) of Bishop Lightfoot, who with his characteristic generosity had undertaken to bear the cost of its publication at the Cambridge Press".

As regards Dr Lambros, all I want is permission to print the extracts (a line or two) out of his Catalogue. Could you get this for me?

The [other][1] is a more difficult matter. The gain is not likely to be considerable, or worth much outlay, but if anyone were going there on his own errand, and could do mine also, I should be glad. I have written to Dr Hort about Gregory. Have you anyone to suggest?

June 15, 1887.

In Reimar's note on Dion Cass. LXVII, 14 there is a reference to an Inscription running DOMITILLA. CONJVX. SATRI. SILONIS. NEPTIS. VESPESANI. IM. which is to be found "apud Jo. Vig-nolium in Inscriptt. p. 318".

Would you please look at the book itself (I think the title is *Vignolius De Columna Imperatoris Antonini Pii*, Romae 1705), and see how it is, and where it is?

I cannot find it in any of the ordinary Collections of Inscriptions, and suspect it is spurious.

I am looking forward to seeing you on St Peter's Day.

July 19, 1887.

(1) Would you be good enough to look out the *1st series* of De Rossi's *Bollettino di Archeologia Cristiana* in the University Library, and take it to Macmillans, directing them to send it to me without delay. It is, I think, bound in a single volume.

(2) Also would you look at Mionnet Supplement VI, 324 (I sup-pose this is the number of the page) and copy out the legend and de-scription of the coin or coins (Smyrnæan) which bear the proper name ΚΛΗΤΟΣ.

(3) I do not know quite what to do about Sp. Lambros. Would it be sufficient to send him:

    (a) Funk's *second* vol. of *Patr. Apost.* I believe the vols. are sold separately;

    (b) *Patres Apost.* (Gebhardt, Harnack and Zahn *Editio Minor*)?

[1] The word "other" above is scarcely legible. As a rule the Bishop wrote a very good hand, but sometimes a familiar word would have the first three letters well written and the rest a wavy line. Once the manuscript of a sermon on St Luke x. 7 was sent to a local printer and came back in proof headed "The Cabman is worthy of his hire".

These two contain everything and much more than he would want. And they are convenient and portable and they answer every purpose. If you think this would be sufficient please tell Deightons, not Macmillans, with whom I have a bill, to put them up and send them as you may direct, charging me with the cost of the books, and postage—in short all expenses.

I am sorry to give you so much trouble. If there is anything in this which won't work—tell me so, or alter it at your discretion, and be sure to thank Dr Lambros for me.

My foreign friends, one and all, either accept, or regard as highly probable, my discovery of Hegesippus' Papal List in Epiphanius—which you may have seen in *The Academy* a few weeks ago.

I shall have to send the parts of my Ignatius and Polycarp which will be affected by these collations to the press for the new edition before the end of the year at the latest.

Would it expedite matters to offer remuneration for the trouble of collating? I am not prepared to pay travelling expenses.

July 31, 1887.

I am much obliged to you for the trouble you have taken on my behalf. Everything was done as I desired.

Thanks also for directing my attention to the other passage of Epiphanius. When I mentioned my view of the Papal List to Dr Hort he expressed the opinion that Epiphanius was elsewhere indebted to Hegesippus. The passage which you point out is a case in point. I had reserved the investigation of the portion of Epiphanius relating to the Judaising Sects till a convenient season, hoping that I might track out some other obligations, but I have never found the leisure, and meanwhile you have anticipated me.

I was much grieved to hear of your loss, of which I was unaware when I wrote to you. Otherwise I don't think I should have ventured to trouble you.

We had a very successful day at Lichfield, and "Prebendary" Southwell[1] is delighted with the success of the reunion. The day before

---

[1] His Chaplain, Rev. H. B. Southwell, had just been appointed Principal of Lichfield Theological College, and made a Prebendary of the Cathedral.

I tied the knot for Willink[1] in quite an ideal Church of an ideal village near Dorking.

I leave for Norway to-morrow.

May 1, 1888.

(1) Can you find out at your leisure the volume, or year, of the *Journal of the Exegetical Society* which contains Rendel Harris' "Ignatiana", p. 90? I have the paper detached, but want the reference to the volume.

(2) Do you think there is any chance of my getting the collation of the *Martyrdom of Polycarp* or the *Acts of Ignatius* from Athos before the end of June, the former more especially? If so, I think I should keep back those sheets. Something *might* come out of the *Martyrdom of Polycarp*.

(3) I asked Harmer to write to you at Athens, and ask to whom you had sent presentation copies of your Hermas that I might avoid them, more especially foreign scholars.

Your conclusions on the main points seem to me to be quite decisive. I shall be curious to hear when we meet what you say about Arcadia. I confess to a certain predisposition towards the Arcadian Theory.

I am off to Dublin in less than an hour, to receive a degree, and in consequence am writing in a great hurry.

[1] Rev. J. W. Willink, afterwards Dean of Norwich.

Appendix B

THE AUCKLAND BROTHERHOOD

E = Easter, M = Michaelmas, L = Lent, T = Trinity *and indicates First Term at Auckland*, * = Chaplain, † = Lecturer.

E 1879 EDEN, George Rodney, D.D., Pemb. Coll. Cam.*[1]
         SAVAGE, Henry Edwin, D.D., C.C.C. Cam.*[2]
M 1879 EDEN, Frederick Nugent, M.A., Pemb. Coll. Cam.
         COPE, Frederick Lorance, M.A., Pemb. Coll. Cam.
         GLYN, Frederick Ware, M.A., Keble Coll. Oxf.
E 1880 GUY, Douglas Sherwood, B.D., Trin. Coll. Cam.†
         JEPSON, George, M.A., Caius Coll. Cam.
         COATES, Charles Hutton, M.A., Trin. Coll. Cam.
         ELMHIRST, William Heaton, B.A., Jesus Coll. Cam.
M 1880 GIBSON, Reginald Daniell, M.A., Trin. Coll. Cam.
         COBBOLD, Francis Edward D., M.A., Pemb. Coll. Cam.
L 1881 WILLINK, John Wakefield, D.D.(Lambeth), Pemb. Coll. Cam.[3]
E 1881 WAWN, Arnold Dykes, M.A., Jesus Coll. Cam.
         HARMER, John Reginald, D.D., King's and C.C.C. Cam.*[4]
M 1881 SOUTHWELL, Herbert Burrows, M.A., Pemb. Coll. Oxf.*
         FFOULKES, Piers John B., M.A., Keble Coll. Oxf.
         WARD, Walter Francis B., M.A., Keble Coll. Oxf.
         WOOD, John Stevenson C., B.A., Trin. Coll. Cam.
         BANTON, Herbert Rider, M.A., Jesus Coll. Cam.*
         BULL, Reginald Alfred, M.A., Trin. Coll. Cam.
L 1882 GORE BROWNE, Wilfrid, M.A., Trin. Coll. Cam.[5]
         DERRY, Percy Augustus, M.A., Trin. Coll. Oxf.[6]

[1] Bishop of Dover, 1890–1897; Bishop of Wakefield, 1897–1928.
[2] Dean of Lichfield, 1909–   .
[3] Dean of Norwich, 1919–1928.
[4] Bishop of Adelaide, 1895–1905; Bishop of Rochester, 1905–1930.
[5] Bishop of Kimberley and Kuruman, 1912–1928.
[6] Archdeacon of Auckland, 1914–1929.

M 1882 JUPP, William Theodore, M.A., Ch. Ch. Oxf.
LAMBERT, Edgar, M.A., Pemb. Coll. Cam.
DINGLE, Arthur Trehane, M.A., Ch. Ch. Oxf.
BODDINGTON, Edgar, M.A., Jesus Coll. Cam.
L 1883 APPLETON, Arthur, M.A., Trin. Coll. Cam.
HEDLEY, Herbert, M.A., Trin. Coll. Cam.
M 1883 ROBINSON, Joseph Armitage, D.D., Christ's Coll. Cam.*[1]
FRASER, Alexander Campbell, M.A., Edin. and Oriel
Coll. Oxf.
ROWLEY, Herbert Seddon, M.A., Queen's Coll. Oxf.
WELLDON, Charles Edward, M.A., Keble Coll. Oxf.
MACKINTOSH, Alexander, M.A., St John's Coll. Cam.
L 1884 KING, George Lanchester, D.D., Clare Coll. Cam.[2]
LAW, James Henry Adeane, M.A., Trin. Coll. Cam.
MACDONALD, Frederick Charles, M.A., Oriel Coll. Oxf.
SMYTH, Arthur Worsley, M.A., Trin. Coll. Cam.
E 1884 McMASTER, Acheson Archibald, M.A., Pemb. Coll. Cam.
CURTOYS, William Francis D., M.A., Oriel Coll. Oxf.
M 1884 HUBAND, Hugo Richard, M.A., Trin. Coll. Cam.
KYNASTON, William Herbert, B.A., St John's Coll. Cam.
SIM, Arthur Fraser, M.A., Pemb. Coll. Cam.
NORRIS, Charles Leslie, M.A., New Coll. Oxf.
L 1885 STEWART, Edward Hamilton, M.A., Trin. Coll. Cam.
WESTCOTT, Foss, D.D., Peterhouse, Cam.[3]
SYKES, Edward, M.A., Trin. Coll. Cam.
E 1885 EVERY, Edward Francis, D.D., Trin. Coll. Cam.[4]
M 1885 BALL, Frederick, M.A., Exeter Coll. Oxf.
BARTLETT, William, M.A. C.C.C. Oxf.
BOWEN, Hon. William Edward, M.A., Balliol Coll. Oxf.
PYBUS, George, M.A., Peterhouse, Cam.
SLACK, Austin Ainsworth, M.A., Pemb. Coll. Cam.
L 1886 SOMERS-COCKS, Henry Lawrence, M.A., Trin. Coll. Cam.

[1] Dean of Westminster, 1902–1911; Dean of Wells, 1911–   .
[2] Bishop in Madagascar, 1899–1919; Assistant Bishop of Rochester, 1928–   .
[3] Bishop of Chota Nagpur, 1905–1919; Bishop of Calcutta and Metropolitan, 1919–   .
[4] Bishop of Falkland Isles, 1902–1910; Bishop in Argentina and E. South America, 1910–   .

E 1886 CLARK, Edward, M.A., New Coll. Oxf.
M 1886 CHATTERTON, Eyre, D.D., Trin. Coll. Dublin.[1]
         DOBINSON, Henry Hughes, M.A., B.N.C. Oxf.[2]
         HARDING, Thomas Williamson, M.A., St John's Coll.
         Cam.
         KIRBY, Edward, M.A., C.C.C., Oxf.
L 1887 WELCH, Edward Ashurst, D.C.L., King's Coll. Cam.*[3]
         BURN, Andrew Ewbank, D.D., Trin. Coll. Cam.[4]
         FELL, James, M.A., Pemb. Coll. Cam.
E 1887 AMOS, Andrew, M.A., Clare Coll. Cam.
         FORD, Alfred Henry, M.A., Univ. Coll. Durham
         LEAKE, Francis Aubrey Eyton, B.A., St John's Coll.
         Cam.
         LITTLE, Thomas Wright, M.A., King's Coll. Cam.
M 1887 BAILLIE, Albert Victor, D.D., Trin. Coll. Cam.[5]
         BOUTFLOWER, Cecil Henry, D.D., Ch. Ch. Oxf.*[6]
         GREGSON, Francis Sitwell Knight, M.A., B.N.C. Oxf.[7]
         MACKENZIE, John George Kenneth, M.A., New Coll.
         Oxf.
         ROLT, Cecil Henry, M.A., New Coll. Oxf.[8]
L 1888 ADAMS, Reginald Arthur, M.A., Pemb. Coll. Cam.[9]
         BRISTOW, James Berkeley, B.D., Trin. Coll. Dublin.
E 1888 HUNTINGTON, Henry Edward, M.A., Keble Coll. Oxf.
M 1888 BROWN, George Gibson, M.A. Edin., M.A. Balliol Coll.
         Oxf.
         HUNT, Reginald Coombs, M.A., Wadh. Coll. Oxf.
         KEMPTHORNE, John Augustine, D.D., Trin. Coll. Cam.[10]
         KINLOCH, Michael Ward, M.A., Pemb. Coll. Cam.
L 1889 BABER, Francis Villiers, B.A., Ball. Coll. Oxf.

[1] Bishop of Nagpur, 1903–1926.
[2] Archdeacon of the Niger, 1896–1897.
[3] Provost Trin. Coll. Toronto, Chancellor of Cathedral, 1895–1899.
[4] Dean of Salisbury, 1921–1927.
[5] Dean of Windsor, 1917–   .
[6] Bishop of Dorking, 1905–1909. Bishop of Tokyo, 1909–1921. Bishop
of Southampton, 1921–   .
[7] Archdeacon of Natal, 1908–1914.
[8] Dean of Capetown, 1917–1924.
[9] Archdeacon of Willochra, 1924–1927.
[10] Bishop of Hull, 1910–1913; Bishop of Lichfield, 1913–   .

L 1889 COLLET, Mark Cubbon Humphrys, M.A., Trin. Hall, Cam.

CRAWFURD, Lionel Payne, D.D., Ball. Coll. Oxf.[1]

GLENNIE, Reginald Gerard, M.A., Keble Coll. Oxf.

SCOTT, George Digby, M.A., Trin. Coll. Cam.

E 1889 PALGRAVE, Francis Milnes Temple, M.A., Trin. Coll. Oxf.

M 1889 HOWE, Henry Arnold, M.A., Univ. Coll. Oxf.

BILBROUGH, Harold Ernest, D.D., New Coll. Oxf.[2]

CRAIG, Oswald, M.A., Emm. Coll. Cam.

L 1891 KNIGHT, Arthur Mesac, D.D., Pemb. Coll. Cam.†[3]

CLARK-MAXWELL, William Gilchrist, M.A., King's Coll. Cam.

HAYES, Ernest William Carlile, M.A., Sid. Suss. Coll. Cam.

SELWYN, William George, M.A., King's Coll. Cam.

WEST, Arthur George Bainbridge, M.A., New Coll. Oxf.

E 1891 HARRISON, William Francis Lightfoot, M.A., Linc. Coll. Oxf.

M 1891 WESTCOTT, Henry, M.A., Pemb. Coll. Cam.*

AITKEN, Arthur William Grant, M.A., Merton Coll. Oxf.

HUDSON, Ernest, M.A., Pemb. Coll. Cam.

L 1892 THOMPSON, Arthur Charles, M.A., St John's Coll. Cam.

E 1892 PURTON, Gerald Astley, M.A., Clare Coll. Cam.

T 1892 FOSTER, Ernest, M.A., New Coll. Oxf.

WATSON, Ralph, M.A., Christ's Coll. Cam.

M 1892 WRIGHT, Arthur Samuel, M.A., New Coll. Oxf.

L 1893 PATTEN, Basil Arthur, M.A., Pemb. Coll. Cam.

PENNEFATHER, William de Montmorency, M.A., Linc. Coll. Oxf.

E 1893 GILLING-LAX, Thomas Graham, M.A., Jesus Coll. Cam.

M 1893 AITKEN, Robert Aubrey, M.A., Merton Coll. Oxf.

BOLTON, Charles Ernest, B.A., Merton Coll. Oxf.

FYFFE, Rollestone Sterritt, D.D., Emm. Coll. Cam.[4]

L 1894 BAX, Arthur Nesham, M.A., Balliol Coll. Oxf.

[1] Bishop of Stafford, 1915–   .
[2] Bishop of Dover, 1916–1927; Bishop of Newcastle, 1927–   .
[3] Bishop of Rangoon, 1903–1909.
[4] Bishop of Rangoon, 1910–1928.

L 1894 PARRY, Oswald Hutton, M.A., Magd. Coll. Oxf.[1]

RAMSBOTHAM, Alexander, M.A., Exeter Coll. Oxf.

M 1894 COCK, Edwin Henry, M.A., Trin. Hall, Cam.

FAWNS, Cecil Anderson, M.A., C.C.C. Cam.

FENNING, Richard Robert, M.A., Pemb. Coll. Cam.

HICHENS, Richard Arthur James, M.A., Exeter Coll. Oxf.

PAINE, William Henry, M.A., Magd. Coll. Oxf.

L 1895 BOVILL, F. H., M.A., Ch. Ch. Oxf.

SMART, Sidney Dallow, M.A., Keble Coll. Oxf.

WARE, Martin Stewart, M.A., Trin. Coll. Cam.

WETHERED, Arthur James, M.A., Ch. Ch. Oxf.

M 1895 LONG, Frederick Percy, M.A., Worcester Coll. Oxf.

MOORE, Daniel Henry, M.A., Trin. Coll. Cam.

PEACOCKE, Philip Græme, M.A., C.C.C. Cam.*

WINDLEY, Henry Chadwick, M.A., King's Coll. Cam.

L 1896 LEWIN, Charles Herbert, M.A., Trin. Coll. Cam.

WALSH, Herbert Pakenham, D.D., Trin. Coll. Dublin.[2]

WIGRAM, William Ainger, B.D., Trin. Hall, Cam., D.D. (Lambeth).

BRYANT, Ernest Edward, M.A., Emm. Coll. Cam.

M 1896 CAMPBELL, George Augustus, M.A., Trin. Coll. Cam.

FLEMING, Herbert James, M.A., Pemb. Coll. Oxf.

FRASER, Keith, M.A., Selwyn Coll. Cam.

L 1897 HORT, Francis Fitzgerald, M.A., Emm. Coll. Cam.

KARNEY, Arthur Baillie Lumsdaine, D.D., Trin. Coll. Cam.[3]

KEELING, Charles Paul, M.A., St John's Coll. Cam.

WANSEY, Henry Raymond, M.A., Univ. Coll. Oxf.

T 1897 ELPHINSTONE, Maurice C., M.A., Trin. Coll. Cam.

SMITH, Herbert Saumarez, M.A., Trin. Coll. Cam.

WIGRAM, Harold Frederick E., M.A., Trin. Coll. Cam.

M 1897 CUMMING-BRUCE, Hon. C. E. H. T., M.A., Trin. Coll. Cam.[4]

L 1898 PAGE, Philip Henry, B.A., Pemb. Coll. Cam.

KNIGHT, Leonard Faulconer Bury, B.A., Univ. Coll. Durham.

---

[1] Bishop of Guiana, 1921– . [2] Bishop of Assam, 1915–1923.
[3] Bishop of Johannesburg, 1922– . [4] Now Baron THURLOW.

L 1898 PERRIN, Howard Nasmith, M.A., King's Coll. Cam.
         WREFORD-BROWN, Gerald, M.A., Oriel Coll. Oxf.*
T 1898 BOLLAND, Ernest Walter, M.A., Oriel Coll. Oxf.
         WARRE-CORNISH, Gerald, B.A., King's Coll. Cam.
M 1898 BAILY, George Herbert Johnson, M.A., Keble Coll. Oxf.
         DOLPHIN, Arthur Rollinson, M.A., Oriel Coll. Oxf.
L 1899 BURNETT, Charles Ridley, M.A., St John's Coll. Oxf.
         GARNETT, Thomas Arthur, M.A., Ch. Ch. Oxf.
T 1899 FORREST, Wilfrid George, B.A., Trin. Coll. Dublin.
         MENZIES, Wilfrid Roxburgh, B.A., Caius Coll. Cam.
         TROLLOPE, Charles Henry B., M.A., Trin. Coll. Cam.
         TURNER, Percy Reginald, M.A., Pemb. Coll. Cam.
M 1899 AUSTEN, Hubert Pearson H., M.A., Keble Coll. Oxf.
         BURGESS, Henry Norman, M.A., St John's Coll. Cam.
L 1900 MOILLIET, Bernard R. Keir, M.A., Pemb. Coll. Oxf.
T 1900 STRONG, Thomas Banks, D.D., Ch. Ch. Oxf.†¹
         WOOD, Charles Travers, M.A., Pemb. Coll. Cam.
M 1900 CHITTY, George Jameson, M.A., King's Coll. Cam.
         KITTERMASTER, Digby Bliss, M.A., Clare Coll. Cam.
L 1901 COWIE, Archibald George Gordon, M.A., Trin. Coll.
         Cam.
         MARTIN, Herbert Craven Lunn, M.A., Clare Coll. Cam.
         DAWSON, Robert Basil, M.A., Merton Coll. Oxf.
E 1901 HUTTON, Martin Burnup, B.A., Caius Coll. Cam.
         CROFT, John Robert, M.A., Queens' Coll. Cam.
M 1901 CAUSTON, Lilford Jervoise, M.A., Pemb. Coll. Cam.*
M 1902 WHATELEY, Walter Richard, M.A., Christ's Coll. Cam.*
         ALLWORTHY, Thomas Bateson, M.A., Christ's Coll. Cam.
         LISTER, Arthur William, M.A., Christ's Coll. Cam.
         MITTON, Launcelot E. Dury, M.A., Pemb. Coll. Cam.
L 1903 CARTER, George Foster, M.A., B.N.C. Oxf.*
M 1903 EDDISON, Frederick William, M.A., Trin. Coll. Cam.*
         BRIERLEY, Joseph Philip Basil, M.A., Queens' Coll. Cam.
         DOUDNEY, Ernest Edward, M.A., Christ's Coll. Cam.
         DRURY, Robert Ferry, M.A., Wadh. Coll. Oxf.
         STORR, Edward Charles, M.A., Pemb. Coll. Cam.
         TAYLOR, Samuel, M.A., Christ's Coll. Cam.

¹ Dean of Christ Church, 1901–1920; Bishop of Ripon, 1920–1925;
Bishop of Oxford, 1925–

L 1904 VENN, Arthur Dennis, M.A., Pemb. Coll. Cam.
M 1904 BUXTON, Harold Jocelyn, M.A., Trin. Coll. Cam.
         LEA-WILSON, Harold Wright, M.A., Trin. Coll. Cam.
         DICKSON, Gerald William, M.A., Trin. Coll. Dublin.
         LISTER, John, M.A., St John's Coll. Cam.
M 1905 LEACH, Robert, M.A., Magdalene Coll. Cam.
         PILCHER, Charles Venn, D.D., Hertford Coll. Oxf.*
M 1906 DE LABILLIERE, Paul Fulcrand, M.A., Merton Coll.
         Oxf.*
         RICHARDSON, Harold Samuel Temple, M.A., Trin. Coll.
         Cam.*
         LASBREY, Ernest William, M.A., Emm. Coll. Cam.
         ROTTON, Hugh Frederick Arthur, M.A., Corpus Coll.
         Cam.
         SUMNER, Cecil Carol Winton, B.A., St John's Coll. Cam.
L 1907 ROTHWELL, Mark Sutton, Ex-Lieutenant R.N.
T 1907 ALFORD, Charles Symes L., M.A., Corpus Coll. Cam.
         BLOWER, Lester Charles, M.A., Christ's Coll. Cam.
         BRADLEY, Arthur Frederic, B.A., Christ's Coll. Cam.
         DIGGES LA TOUCHE, Everard, B.A., T.C.D.
         LUPTON, Reginald Ellison, M.A., Emm. Coll. Cam.
         NIXON, Arthur Lyndon, B.A., Emm. Coll. Cam.
M 1907 PERROTT, Hubert Cecil, M.A., St Edmund Hall, Oxford.
T 1908 LINTON, Robert Cornelius, M.A., Clare Coll. Cam.
         NEWMAN, Rowland Allen Webbe, M.A., Trin. Coll. Cam.
M 1908 WORKMAN, Herbert William, M.A., Pemb. Coll. Cam.*
M 1909 CUSHING, Basil Montague, B.A., Wadham Coll. Oxf.
         THORMAN, Frederick Pelham, B.A., Queens' Coll. Cam.
         BOURDILLON, Gerard Leigh, M.A., Selwyn Coll. Cam.
         CODE, George Brereton, B.A., Pemb. Coll. Cam.
T 1910 CORNFORTH, John William, B.A., Jesus Coll. Oxf.
L 1911 AGLIONBY, John Orfeur, D.D. (Lambeth), Queen's Coll.
         Oxf.¹
M 1911 PETRIE, Stanley Layton, L.Th., Hatfield Hall, Durham.*
         DENHAM, Joseph Percival, M.A., St John's Coll. Cam.
L 1912 HOLLAND, Philip Fielder, B.A., Jesus Coll. Cam.
T 1912 BANHAM, John Clifford, M.A., Trin. Coll. Cam.*

¹ Bishop of Accra, 1924–

T 1912 BETTS, Harold Sidney, M.A., Queens' Coll. Cam.
   READ, Henry Cecil, M.A., Caius Coll. Cam.
M 1913 ALLWORK, Anthony Thomas, M.A., Queen's Coll. Oxf.
   BAILEY, Howard Sinclair, M.A., Queens' Coll. Cam.
   BURTON, Charles Kingsley, M.A., C.C.C. Cam.
   HOOPER, Handley Douglas, M.A., Queens' Coll. Cam.
L 1914 MAISH, Edward Henry, M.A., Queens' Coll. Cam.*
M 1914 THOMAS, Basil Parker, B.A., Queens' Coll. Cam.

Appendix C

DR LIGHTFOOT'S LITERARY PUBLICATIONS

A formal Bibliography of Dr Lightfoot's publications would be out of place in this book of personal Reminiscences, which is not—and does not profess to be—a regular Biography. Moreover, fairly full notices of his works may be consulted both in Dr Hort's account of his life in the *Dictionary of National Biography*, and especially in the Memoir of *Bishop Lightfoot* published anonymously in 1894. It may however be worth while to draw attention to them from a special point of view, as in relation to the circumstances under which they were severally issued; and so to co-ordinate his writings with the successive stages of his career.

For a review of Lightfoot's life-work falls naturally into four clearly defined periods:

    I. 1851–1861: From his B.A. degree to his Professorship.

    II. 1861–1870: His Professoriate.

    III. 1870–1879: The Revision of the New Testament; and his Canonry of St Paul's.

    IV. 1879–1889: Bishop of Durham.

I. In the first decade he published nothing except some articles and reviews in the short-lived (1854–1859) *Journal of Classical and Sacred Philology*. He had been actively interested in the promotion of this Journal; to him was due the inclusion of "Sacred Philology" in its title, as one of its primary objects; and he was one of its joint-editors. For each of its first three years it maintained an annual volume of three parts; but after that, it slowly faded out, with only one part of volume IV in each of the next three years; there being no issue at all between March 1858 and December 1859; after which it ceased. The fate of this Journal is of no particular moment to us in itself, but some of Lightfoot's articles which were published in it were elicited by its urgent need of support, and these have a peculiar interest because of the light that they throw on the trend of his studies in those early years. For his first contribution, in 1854, was purely Classical; a review of two orations of Hyperides, the texts of which had recently been published from some papyri discovered in Egypt. But after that he devoted himself for three years exclusively to St Paul's Epistles; with an Essay on "The Mission of Titus to Corinth",[1] in 1855; a review of "Recent Editions of St Paul's Epistles" (by Ellicott, Stanley and Jowett), in March 1856; a discussion of "The Style and Character of the Epistle to the Galatians", in December 1856; and an article on "They of Caesar's Household" (as illustrated by inscriptions in Rome), in March 1857. Of these the review of the commentaries attracted special attention outside Cambridge, on account of its unsparing criticism of Canon (afterwards Dean) Stanley's edition of the Epistles to the Corinthians.[2]

When, after March 1857, the Journal began to collapse through lack of material, Lightfoot came to its rescue, in March 1858, after it had been quiescent for a year, with a long dissertation on "Some corrupt and obscure passages in the Helena of Euripides". It was however not a fresh composition, but a relic of some former preparation for editing the play. So he himself practically admits in the opening words of his paper: "In transcribing the following notes for publication I have confined myself almost without exception to those passages respecting which I had any conjecture of my own to offer". On the other hand his last contribution to the moribund Journal in December 1859, was written specially for it. It is an extensive note, "On the Long Walls at Athens", which was suggested by a line of Telecleides, quoted by Plutarch (*Vit. Pericl.*), and he writes: "as this application of the passage has never, so far as I am aware, been made, I was anxious to put it forward". Moreover he refers in it to the 1855 edition of Wordsworth's *Attica and Athens*. He had not lost his touch with the Classics. In fact before a year had passed he found himself upon the brink of being driven back upon that as his principal subject. At the time however he was, as these articles shew, concentrating himself more and more on the Greek Testament.

In 1854 Lightfoot was ordained Deacon, on the Title of his Fellowship, by his old Headmaster James Prince Lee, then Bishop of Manchester, who had first inspired him with a keen enthusiasm for Greek Testament study; and he was also ordained Priest by him in 1858. It

---

[1] Reprinted by the Lightfoot Trustees in *Biblical Essays* (1893).

[2] It was this very review that led to Lightfoot's first acquaintance, and subsequent friendship, with Stanley.

would seem that from the time of his Ordination he began to "draw all his cares and studies this way". It was at this period that the Apos-tolic Fathers first engaged his serious attention: "The subject has been before me for nearly thirty years", he wrote, in 1885, in the Preface to his *Ignatius*: but no trace of this interest appears in any of the papers that he published in the Journal. The time was not yet ripe for that; ten years later he was still laboriously working his way through the intricate problems of the genuineness of the Ignatian Epistles, as will appear presently. But in the meantime the Greek Testament, and particularly the Epistles of St Paul, and not least in their historical aspects, con-stituted the focus of his work.

He had already, at this early date, achieved by his College lectures a unique reputation as a lecturer on the Greek Testament. Many years afterwards he himself incidentally revealed how those lectures had attracted larger and larger audiences. In 1877 a Grace was proposed in the Senate for abolishing compulsory attendance at Professors' Lec-tures. Lightfoot at once printed, and circulated, an emphatic protest against this proposition; and in the course of his argument he cited his own experience even before he was a Professor: "During the later courses of my College lecturing, I was obliged to deliver my lectures on Greek Testament twice, because there was no room nearly large enough for my hearers".

When therefore the Hulsean Professorship was founded in 1860, it was generally taken for certain that Lightfoot would be appointed. But the small panel with whom the choice lay elected C. J. Ellicott, then Professor of New Testament Exegesis in King's College, London, and the Hulsean Lecturer of the previous year at Cambridge. It was of course a severe blow to Lightfoot, to be thus obviously put aside; but he modestly interpreted it as an indication that he was now to devote himself to the Classics as his chief subject; and he at once set to work on an edition of the Orestean trilogy of Aeschylus. But that was destined soon to be abandoned.

II. For in the following year Professor Ellicott was appointed Dean of Exeter, and vacated his Professorship; to which Lightfoot was now appointed. And from that time he threw himself entirely into the proper work of his chair.

He now wrote three articles for Smith's *Dictionary of the Bible*, which was published in 1863, on *The Epistle to the Romans*, and on *The First, and The Second, Epistles to the Thessalonians*.

He still held the degree of M.A. Indeed, under the regulations then in force he was not yet eligible to proceed to the D.D. degree, as he had not completed 12 years from taking his M.A. in 1854. But in 1864 a way was found to surmount this difficulty; for on 18 June in that year the D.D. degree was conferred on him by a Grace of the Senate ("by Diploma") under one of the University Statutes;[1] and with him two other Divinity Professors (both of whom had held the M.A. for more than twelve years) were similarly honoured—W. Selwyn, the Lady Margaret Professor, and C. A. Swainson the recently elected Norrisian Professor. (The Regius Professor was already a B.D.) Thenceforward Lightfoot appears as Dr Lightfoot. It was a signal witness to the high regard entertained for him in the University.

Eight months after he received this distinction he published, in February 1865, his first book—*St Paul's Epistle to the Galatians; a Revised Text, with Introduction, Notes, and Dissertations.* It immediately secured a wide and rapid circulation. A second edition was called for in 1866, and three other fresh editions while Dr Lightfoot still remained in Cambridge; to be followed again by four more after he had removed to Durham. He lived, that is, to see it pass through nine editions; and a tenth was issued shortly after his death. And the reason for this eager appreciation is not far to seek; for it opened out a new ideal of what a commentary on a Book of the New Testament could be. In addition to the appeal of the actual exposition, which was not burdened with conflicting interpretations, there were certain features in the scheme of the volume which were novel; among them the examination of the historical setting of the original composition, and the adoption of a specially revised text. Both of these practices are now familiar enough; but they were virtually unknown until Dr Lightfoot introduced their use, now nearly 70 years ago, in his first commentary. In that, his "Introduction, Notes, and Dissertations", each and all contributed to one compact whole. He had worked out his scheme in the practical experience of his lectures.

---

[1] *Stat.*, cap. 3, sec. 5, par. 2. "Iis etiam qui gradum aliquem vel officium aliquod academicum adepti, et loco suo vel ingenio vel propter egregie merita insignes sint, academiae liceat gratiam concedere, ut etiam si non per⸗ fecerint quae per statuta et ordinationes academiae requirantur, ad perfectum gradum admittantur." In the University Registry these Degrees are entered as "Gradus propter merita".

In his Preface to the first edition he stated, "The present work is intended to form part of a complete edition of St Paul's Epistles which, if my plan is ever carried out, will be prefaced by a general introduction and arranged in chronological order". To this purpose he steadfastly adhered for the next three years; and in July 1868 his edition of St Paul's *Epistle to the Philippians* was published as the second instalment of the proposed series.

At this point however that series was interrupted, and no further volume of it was issued until 1875. In the first instance the break was made deliberately by Dr Lightfoot himself. He judged that the time had come to begin the publication of the "complete edition of the Apostolic Fathers" for which he had long been preparing; and at the end of twelve months he brought out his *S. Clement of Rome: The two Epistles to the Corinthians*, in July 1869.

At this time he wrote several articles for the (new) *Journal of Philology*, which had just been started. It may be observed that in 1868 and 1869, while Clement was in his hands, his mind was running on Patristics, as shown by his papers on *Caius or Hippolytus*, and on certain points in *The Ignatian Controversy*; but later in 1869 he reverted to St Paul, in a lengthy discussion of *The Structure and Destination of the Epistle to the Romans* (being a criticism of Renan's *St Paul et sa Mission*). This article had a curious sequel, for two years later it drew from his intimate friend Dr Hort, in the Journal, an elaborate argument concerning the original ending of the Epistle, in which he contested Lightfoot's solution of the problem: and to this Lightfoot in turn replied in the next number, stoutly maintaining his own view.

But more—and more serious—interruptions followed.

III. The Revision of the Authorised Version of the Bible was proposed, and the plans for carrying it out were organised, by the Convocation of Canterbury in 1870; and Dr Lightfoot was invited to join the New Testament Company of Revisers, though he was not a member of Convocation. This invitation he readily accepted; but it was no light task. The labours of the Company lasted from June 1870 to November 1880; and when the Revision of the New Testament was completed it was recorded that "As a rule, a session of four days has been held every month (with the exception of August and September) in each year from the commencement of the work".

When this project of the Revision was announced, and before the New Testament Company had begun its work, Dr Lightfoot was

APPENDIX C

asked to read a paper on the subject to a Clerical Society. Afterwards, in response to a request that the paper might be printed, he expanded it into a book (with an Appendix added on ἐπιούσιος in the Lord's Prayer), and published it, in April 1871, under the title *On a Fresh Revision of the English New Testament*. A second edition was required in less than three months.[1]

Then, in 1871, he was appointed to a Canonry in St Paul's Cathedral. From the first, St Paul's exerted a powerful influence on him, and on his work. It opened out fresh interests, and offered a wider scope for his intensely human sympathies, which had hitherto found expression chiefly in his academic lectures. His powers both of preaching and of lecturing to "all sorts and conditions of men" developed rapidly under this stimulus; and soon he became generally known as a leading teacher with a clear and forcible message. It was inevitable that the demands thus made upon his energies must to some extent interfere with his literary output. But he still resolutely adhered to his larger schemes of publication; and in fact the seven or eight years during which he was a Canon of St Paul's shew a considerable record of achievement.

The nine articles in refutation of the book *Supernatural Religion*, which Dr Lightfoot contributed to the *Contemporary Review* at intervals between December 1874 and May 1877, have already come under notice in this book. In May 1889 he republished them as a book, in which he included a further article, not of that series, which had appeared in the same Review in May 1878, on *Discoveries illustrating The Acts of the Apostles*.

In April 1875 he issued his edition of *St Paul's Epistles to the Colossians and to Philemon*, which met with a notable reception: it reached its fifth edition by 1880, and its tenth by 1882.

When Lightfoot published *S. Clement of Rome* in 1869 there was only one, imperfect, MS. of the two Epistles known—in the "Codex Alexandrinus" (= A) at the British Museum. At the end of 1875 however the Metropolitan Bryennios published a complete text of both

---

[1] When the Revised Version of the New Testament was published in May 1881, Canon F. C. Cook at once issued *A Protest against the Change in the Last Petition of the Lord's Prayer*. Bishop Lightfoot promptly took up his challenge with an elaborate article which appeared in *The Guardian* in September. This was reprinted after his death in the third edition (1891) of his book *On a Fresh Revision*.

the Epistles from a MS. at Constantinople; and early in 1876 the Cambridge University Library purchased a MS. of the Syriac New Testament which on examination was found to include in the Canon the two Epistles of Clement. In the light therefore of these important accessions of textual matter Dr Lightfoot promptly set about pre-paring a second volume of Clement, which he published (on his 49th birthday) in April 1877, as an "Appendix" to the former book.

It was about this time that he contributed a remarkable article on *Eusebius of Caesarea* to the *Dictionary of Christian Biography* (the second volume, in which it appears, was published in 1880). Of this, Bishop A. Robertson, himself an eminent authority on Eusebius, wrote: "Lightfoot's article is a magnificent monument of patristic scholarship and contains the best and most exhaustive treatment of the life and writings of Eusebius that has been written".[1]

The fulness of this treatise may be associated with the abandonment by Dr Lightfoot of his former "project of a history of Early Christian Literature" to which he refers in the Preface to his "*Appendix*" *to Clement of Rome* (p. vi). With that project in view, he explains, he had deliberately refrained in his book of 1869 from discussing the personal origin of Clement; but as it had since been set aside, he could now, in 1877, deal with the question.

There was also an article by him on *The Acts of the Apostles*, the composition of which must almost certainly be ascribed to this period of his life. It was written for a re-edition of the first volume of Smith's *Dictionary of the Bible*. In that Dictionary as at first issued several of the earlier articles were quite inadequate—for instance, only three columns were allotted to *Acts*—and it was decided to reconstitute volume I on the fuller scale of the two other volumes. This revision was not pub-lished until April 1893; but after Dr Lightfoot was consecrated Bishop there was no year in which it could have been possible for him to prepare this work; especially with the constant claim of *The Apostolic Fathers* pressing upon him. Moreover his paper in the *Contemporary Review* on *Discoveries illustrating the Acts* suggests that he was engaged on the subject in 1878.

IV. With his removal to Durham in 1879 there came the great breach in the tenor of his work. It was no longer possible, as it had

---

[1] Select Library of Nicene and Post-Nicene Fathers: *Eusebius*, p. 3 (1890).

been at St Paul's, to combine his various schemes of literary production with the new claims upon his energies, for the diocese demanded his whole-hearted devotion, and he gave it ungrudgingly.

He did, however, when weighing this great sacrifice, make the one tentative reservation of his "magnum opus", *The Apostolic Fathers*. His edition of *Ignatius and Polycarp* was already well advanced before he left Cambridge; and he cherished the hope that he might be able, by a scrupulous use of any intervals of comparative leisure which should occur, to bring it to completion; but six and a half years passed before he could publish his masterpiece, in 1885. This great work, although it could only appeal directly to scholars, was so widely welcomed that within four years a second edition was required, in 1889.

When this had been completed the Bishop returned once more to *Clement*, and began to prepare a thorough revision of his former volumes, on the same scale as his *Ignatius*. But a severe illness supervened, and, in spite of heroic efforts, he was unable quite to finish it. The two, greatly enlarged, volumes were published in 1890, a few months after his death, just as he had left them.

It was while this task was in his hands that he published in *The Academy* of May 21st, 1887 a paper on *The Lost List of Hegesippus*.[1] It was his practice when he made an important discovery to announce it forthwith in some literary periodical, in order to elicit the opinions of other investigators.

An instance of a somewhat analogous publication of a new proposition is his article in *The Academy* of Sept. 21st, 1889, on *The Muratorian Fragment*, in which he argued that it was originally composed in Greek iambics. This paper however, having little or no connexion with the work on which he was engaged at the time, seems to fall into a different category, as intended to put on record, while his life lasted, a discovery of earlier years that he considered worthy of preservation.

For similarly in the early months of that year he had published in *The Expositor* a Lecture on the *Internal Evidence for the Authenticity and Genuineness of St John's Gospel*,[2] which he had delivered in 1871 as "one of a series connected with Christian evidences" by different Lecturers. He had withheld it at the time from publication, with the design of amplifying it; but now, as he had found no opportunity of

---

[1] Cp. *S. Clement of Rome* (1890), i, 327. See above, p. 164.
[2] Reprinted in *Biblical Essays* (1893).

fulfilling this purpose, he printed it in its original form, to witness that he had never seen reason to modify his judgment of that Gospel.

So also in 1889, as has already been noticed, he re-issued his articles on *Supernatural Religion* in book form.

The useful edition of the text of *The Apostolic Fathers*, with translations, in one volume, was projected by the Bishop himself in these last months of his life. It was his final contribution to the study of this literature, by making it readily accessible to general readers. He settled the plan of the book; he selected the writings to be included in it; and he began the actual preparation of it. But when his strength failed he commissioned his Chaplain, the Rev. J. R. Harmer, to take charge of the work and complete it as Editor. It was published in 1891.

Apart from these publications, which were devoted to the completion of work that was already in progress when he was called to Durham, the Bishop was unable to undertake any further literary work. His whole time was absorbed by the administration of his diocese, as he explained in his second Visitation Charge in 1886. Indeed both that and his earlier Charge of 1882 were confined to reviewing the progress of the diocese in the preceding four years. And publications of this nature do not come within the purview of the present sketch; especially as their relation to the circumstances of his career is patent.

Yet in all that he printed in these years the underlying force of his scholarship, and of his historical acumen, is manifest, and in some instances it is the dominant feature; as when, for example, in a paper read at the Carlisle Church Congress in 1884, on *Results of Recent Historical and Topographical Research*, he gave his first impressions of the newly-discovered *Epitaph of Abercius*, and of the *Didache*.

With respect however to one class of his writings Dr Lightfoot never hesitated about publication. From his ordination onwards he had been accustomed from time to time to print as separate pamphlets sermons that he preached on special occasions; not so much for general circulation, as for the benefit of those who were interested in the particular occasions. The earliest of these pamphlets now traceable is a Commemoration Sermon preached in Trinity College Chapel on 15 Dec. 1860. In process of time, as Lightfoot's influence extended, more and more of them were printed.

But such isolated publications naturally tend to disappear; and in fact they are now rarely to be found. The Trustees of the Lightfoot Fund, therefore, shortly after the Bishop's death, published six volumes of selections from his *Sermons* and *Addresses*. These include some which had already been published separately; with many others, which had not been printed, from his MSS. then in the possession of the Trustees.

These collections are:

Ordination Addresses (1890): to Ordination Candidates; to the Auckland Brotherhood; and to Oxford Fellows in Retreat at Cuddesdon.

Leaders in the Northern Church (1890). The one series of sermons which Lightfoot contemplated issuing together in a volume, when complete, was of those which dealt with the past history of the diocese. He planned it to consist of fourteen such sermons; but had only found appropriate occasions for ten of his proposed subjects before his death. These ten are published in this book. (These first two books belong entirely to the Durham period. The following are drawn partly from the earlier periods also; as indicated by the range of dates of the items, given in brackets.)

Cambridge Sermons (1890): in Trinity College Chapel (1861–1875); and before the University (1868–1883).

Sermons on Special Occasions (1891). (1872–1888.)

Sermons in St Paul's (1891). (1871–1879.)

Historical Essays (1895). (1872–1889.)

These posthumous publications have a peculiar value, as revealing the Preacher and the Lecturer in contact with his audiences. Without them he would have been known as a great Scholar, and a great Organiser. But they portray him, though all unconsciously, by his own words, as the great modern 'Leader in the Northern Church'.

H. E. S.

PUBLISHED AFTER HIS DEATH

"I BELIEVE FROM MY HEART THAT THE
TRUTH WHICH THIS (ST JOHN'S) GOSPEL
MORE ESPECIALLY ENSHRINES—THE TRUTH
THAT JESUS CHRIST IS THE VERY WORD
INCARNATE, THE MANIFESTATION OF THE
FATHER TO MANKIND—IS THE ONE LESSON
WHICH DULY APPREHENDED WILL DO MORE
THAN ALL OUR FEEBLE EFFORTS TO PURIFY
AND ELEVATE HUMAN LIFE HERE BY IM-
PARTING TO IT HOPE, AND LIGHT AND
STRENGTH; THE ONE STUDY WHICH ALONE
CAN FITLY PREPARE US FOR A JOYFUL
IMMORTALITY HEREAFTER."

Biblical Essays, p. 44

INDEX

Abercius, 119, 160, 182
Academy, The, 164, 181
Acts of Apostles, "a forgery", 128;
  genuineness, 140, 179, 180;
  lectures on, 129
Aeschylus, 5, 6, 123, 176
Ahrens, 162
Aidan, St, 69, 73, 89, 98
Aldhun, Bishop, 19
Analecta Solesmensia, 161
ἀνδρίζεσθε κραταιοῦσθε, 52, 103
Apostolic Fathers, 53, 57, 107, 120,
  130, 137, 153, 154, 176, 180
Arabic, knowledge of, 118
Arcadian theory, 165
Armenian, knowledge of, 118,
  129
Asia Minor cities, sites of, 161
Asia Minor discoveries, 119
Athens, 165, 175
Athos, Mt, 162
Auckland Archdeaconry, 129
Auckland Brotherhood, xi, 22, 23,
  48, 157
Auckland Castle, ix, 16, 22, 23,
  96, 160; Chapel of, 24, 35, 39,
  40, 46, 70, 72; life at, 24,
  35–41; monograph on, 111;
  portrait-window, 73, 93
Auckland "Family", origin of, 32
Auckland Manor House, 72, 111
Auckland Park, 16, 29, 70, 109
αὐτάρκεια, 134

Banton, Rev. H. R., 24, 51, 80
Barber, Mr Joseph, bookseller, 1
Barbour, Dr Freeland, 34
Barbour, Rev. R. W., 34
Baring, Bishop, xiv, 59, 107
Baur, Ferdinand C., 128, 138
Bede, Ven., 98, 100, 158; *Eccles.
  History*, 90
Benefices doubled, 59

Benson, Archbishop, ix, 2, 12, 19,
  45, 49, 101, 102
Benwell Tower, 61
Birkbeck Lecturer, 137
Birmingham, 2, 149
Bishop Auckland, 24, 35
"Bishoprick, the", 62, 156
Bishoprics Bill (1878), 59
Boddington, Rev. E., 89 f.
Body, Canon, 27, 48, 68, 81
Bollettino di Archeologia Cristiana,
  163
Bollig, Dr, 54
Boutflower, Bishop, xi
Boys, promising, 66, 69–71
Braemar, 45, 121
Browne, Bishop (Forrest), x, 90
Browne, Bishop (Harold), 18
Bryennios, 27, 54, 179
Bury, Bishop De, scholarship
  founded, 112
Butler, Bishop, ix n., 97, 158

Caesar's Household, 175
Caius or Hippolytus, 178
Cambridge, Great St Mary's, 15;
  King's College, 122; Master of
  Trinity, 4 n., 18, 123, 125
Cambridge Review, 3 n., 14 n.
Carlisle Church Congress, 160
Castle choirboys, 69–71, 122
Catacombs, 119, 175
Chanticleer, Bishop's article in, 24
Chaplains, Domestic, 16, 113;
  Examining, 19, 77; Honorary,
  86
Chapter House restoration, 55, 94
Charges, Primary, 116; Second
  Quadrennial, 66, 71
Christian Literature, History of, 140
Church Assembly foreshadowed, 63
Church building, 121
Church Congress, 60, 115

For EU product safety concerns, contact us at Calle de José Abascal, 56–1°,
28003 Madrid, Spain or eugpsr@cambridge.org.

www.ingramcontent.com/pod-product-compliance
Ingram Content Group UK Ltd.
Pitfield, Milton Keynes, MK11 3LW, UK
UKHW040616240426
470322UK00010B/155